Rüdiger Liedtke

111 Places
in Mallorca
That You
Shouldn't Miss

111

T0344255

emons:

© Emons Verlag GmbH
All rights reserved
All photographs © Rüdiger Liedtke, except:
ch 5 bottom: Fundación Yannick y Ben Jakober;
ch. 88 bottom: Finca Pescador
Cover icon: shutterstock.com/mikecphoto
Layout: Eva Kraskes, based on a design
by Lübbeke | Naumann | Thoben
Maps: altancicek.design, www.altancicek.de
Basic cartographical information from Openstreetmap,
© OpenStreetMap-Mitwirkende, OdbL
Translated by: Tom Ashforth
Editing: Ros Horton
Printing and binding: Grafisches Centrum Cuno, Calbe
Printed in Germany 2021
ISBN 978-3-7408-1049-8
Revised new edition, February 2021

Did you enjoy this guidebook? Would you like to see more?
Join us in uncovering new places around the world on:
www.111places..com

Foreword

Did you know that you can scale a roof of God in Palma, that an unusual donkey awaits you in the Tramuntana mountain range, that an eldorado for cyclists beckons in Alaró and an encounter with Rafa Nadal is in store in Manacor? That there are piano evenings without pianists in S'Alqueria Blanca, that Can Picafort is a stronghold for graffiti, that you can trace the lives of well-to-do gentlemen from past centuries in Palma or experience Mallorca from its wildest side on Cap Blanc? Do you know the cross of Mallorca? And the most mysterious monastery on the island? With around 200 monasteries and hermitages, Mallorca has the highest concentration of spiritual places in the whole of Europe, and in Palma a nativity scene with more than a thousand figures is surely one of Europe's largest.

Mallorca is much more than sun, sea and partying. The island is incredibly diverse. There is mass tourism *and* exclusive five-star hotels, pedalos *and* luxury yachts, beach tennis *and* eighteen-hole golf courses. Mallorca has been shaped by a turbulent history and a cultural diversity the like of which you would be hard pushed to find anywhere else. On top of all this, there's the unique landscape and one of Europe's most attractive metropolises, Palma. Anyone who has properly understood what Mallorca has to offer, will never again speak disparagingly of it simply being a 'party island'.

This is a new edition of *111 Places in Mallorca That You Shouldn't Miss*. The book has been completely reworked and updated. There are dozens of new and exciting places that will leave you awestruck, and some real journeys of discovery. Once again, even Mallorca aficionados will be taken to places that will surprise them, far from all the hustle and bustle of tourism. And not just once, but 111 times over.

111 Places

1__ Castell Miquel Vineyard

Viniculture on the slopes of the Tramuntana range

The journey here is itself a pleasure. As you pass the mighty and strange massifs of d'Alaró and de s'Alcadena and snake through the vineyards, you can already see the lettering 'Castell Miquel' from far off, on an elongated building high on the mountain with the white castle in front of it. The latter is the residence of the German pharmaceutical entrepreneur Prof. Dr Michael Popp, who has set up a vineyard here and created wines in recent years that have made this a top address on the island and much more than just an insider tip.

The family-owned pharmaceutical company Bionorica from the Bavarian town of Neumarkt, which specialises in natural medicinal compounds and has had a bestseller in its range for years with 'Sinupret', has grown medicinal plants on Mallorca for 20 years due to the excellent climate, and runs a processing company in Consell. At some point Michael Popp came upon the idea of buying the semi-derelict Es Castellet estate in the Tramuntana mountain range, to revive wine growing here following scientific methods. Wine as a health elixir so to speak, produced organically. The former stables were converted into barrel storage rooms, maturing cellars and production halls. Today, the wine terraces of Castell Miquel with their Shiraz, Merlot and Cabernet Sauvignon vines are among the most exclusive slopes on Mallorca, as the names of some of the Castell Miquel wines attest: 'Stairway to Heaven', 'Pearls of an Angel' or 'Monte Sion'. The bodega is run by a vintner from the Palatinate region of Germany.

Castell Miquel has no restaurant, but offers regular wine tastings. Parties and events are also arranged on the bodega's wide terraces, predominantly however by the company Bionorica, when it's all about making new plant-based medicines attractive, especially to German pharmacists.

Address Bodegas Castell Miquel, Carretera Alaró–Lloseta, 07340 Alaró, +34 (0)971 510698, www.castellmiquel.com | **Getting there** Palma Ma-13 towards Inca–Port d'Alcúdia, exit Consell/Binissalem, then towards Alaró, before you reach the middle of town head towards Lloseta, at kilometre 8.7 follow the sign to 'Bodega' | **Hours** Apr–Oct Mon–Fri noon–7pm, Sat 11am–2pm; Nov–Mar Mon–Fri 10am–5pm (with wine sales) | **Tip** The José L. Ferrer vineyard in Binissalem with adjoining wine museum and a chance to view and taste is worth a visit.

2_ The Cycling Eldorado
In preparation for a grand tour

Last exit Alaró. Cycling on Mallorca has been hip for years, more so than in any other holiday destination in Europe. On the plains of the island's interior, in the hilly landscapes of Llevant, to monasteries and remote churches, to coasts and bays, but especially in the peaks of the Tramuntana mountain range. There are challenges and adventures in equally beautiful landscapes. Mallorca is a paradise for cycling fans, whether they be the racing, mountain or touring bike variety.

Before heading out and up to the summits of the Tramuntana range, many cyclists get kitted out and tuned up in Alaró. Here a real professional awaits, in a quaint shop on the main street: Cycling Planet. David Muntaner, born and bred Mallorquin, multiple Spanish champion, track racing world champion and national racing bike idol, opened this shop in 2012 while still pursuing a successful cycling career. Since hanging up his jersey in 2015, he has stood on the shop floor and his approachable manner really sets the tone at Cycling Planet. He is assisted in the venture by his racing bike brother Alberto and other cycling experts. It's no surprise that the top teams who pitch up their training camps on Mallorca stop by here, just like anyone who knows anything about the bicycle business.

It is, alongside all of the cycling professionalism – brand bikes, equipment, special nutrition, repairs and mechanics, rentals, professional clothing, route maps and advice – the flair that makes this shop distinctive, not only for cycling enthusiasts. Between the sales area, bicycle rentals and workshop there's a lively café, mainly frequented by cyclists who are about to set off for the Tramuntana mountains or who are just taking a break here. The boss' racing bikes hang on the walls, alongside team jerseys and unusual accessories from cycling celebrities who have passed by here over the years.

Address Cycling Planet, Avenue Constitutió 26, 07340 Alaró, +34 (0)971 510691 or +34 (0)640 769416 | **Getting there** From Palma Ma-13 towards Inca–Port d'Alcudia, exit Consell/Binissalem, then on to Alaró | **Hours** Mon–Fri 9am–8pm, Sat & Sun 9am–2pm | **Tip** One of the most popular destinations for cyclists is Castell d'Alaró on the 600-metre-high Puig d'Alaró, which can't be reached by car. There are now many trendy bike shops on the island, especially in Palma. A first address: Rapha on Plaça del Rosari.

3 The 13th Hole

Teeing off to the island

You don't have to be a golfer to enjoy this idyllic place. The unbelievable views, the fresh air, the great greens and a good restaurant with an extensive terrace make a visit to Alcanada Golf Club a real pleasure.

The club house and restaurant are housed in an old finca. Here you can enjoy a bite to eat or have a drink. Scenically located on the peninsula of La Victòria in north-east Mallorca – experts say that this golf course, which opened in 2003, is the most beautiful on the Balearic Islands – this sanctuary, far from all the hustle and bustle, is a real insider tip.

The course is vast and generously laid out, stretching deep into the island's interior. It is hilly and slopes down towards the sea and is surrounded by a nature reserve located directly by the sea, offering a view of the bay of Alcúdia in the distance and the mountain panorama of Sierra de Llevant – and especially the little island of Alcanada.

This small island with its white lighthouse, which is still in operation, stands below the golf club, around 100 metres off the coast. Those who want to reach the island have to swim, wade through the water on foot or bring a boat. When teeing off from the 13th hole, assuming you strike it well, the ball seems to fly for an eternity towards the lighthouse.

The almost 7-kilometre-long, 18-hole Alcanada course, laid out by American golf course designer Robert Trent Jones Jr, far away from any building development and any kind of source of noise, is one of over two dozen more or less exquisite golf courses on Mallorca, most of which are in close proximity to Palma.

All of the courses here are bookable and playable all year round simply by paying the green fee, without having to pay for any kind of membership.

Address Club de Golf Alcanada, Carretera del Faro–Alcanada, 07400 Port d'Alcúdia, +34 (0)971 549560, www.golf-alcanada.com | **Getting there** From Alcúdia the Ma-3460 and then in Port d'Alcúdia towards Alcanada; bus L 356 departs from Port d'Alcúdia | **Hours** All year, almost daily 8am–dusk | **Tip** It's worth taking a look at the ruins of the mega club Es Fogueró Palace in Port d'Alcúdia on the Ma-3470/corner of Ma-3433 opposite Urb. Can Lloreta, a party temple of superlatives for 2,000 people, which was opened in 1989 by Julio Iglesias, but closed only four years later and is now deserted.

4 Can Torró Library

Bertelsmann invests on Mallorca

The Mohn family from Gütersloh in Germany, who own the media company Bertelsmann which consists of the publisher Random House, the television channel RTL and *Stern* magazine, has had a soft spot for Mallorca for decades, and owns an impressive property near Alcúdia.

As the publishing group has always done good business in Spain – the Spanish book club Círculo de Lectores was one of their most profitable businesses for years – the Mohns decided to build themselves a lasting monument in Alcúdia. Based on the archetype of the city library in Gütersloh, a model library initiated by the in-house Bertelsmann foundation at the family's headquarters, the Can Torró library was founded in Alcúdia in 1989.

The radically restored historical Casal Can Torró, which houses the library, is located in the middle of the old town and has developed into one of the cultural centres of north-east Mallorca. The three storeys of Can Torró are not only a classical library and a place for promoting reading, but the place has invested heavily in multimedia activities, which are very well received especially among schoolchildren and students. Alongside the classic literature there are newspapers and magazines, games of all kinds and numerous well-equipped computer stations, where you can surf the internet or check your e-mails. Can Torró has become a business meeting place in Alcúdia, but also a place of relaxation. Especially inviting is the large patio in the courtyard.

Since 1997 the City of Alcúdia has had sole responsibility for Can Torró. But the Bertelsmann foundation is still represented with three people on the library's foundation board of seven. The Fundacíon Bertelsmann, a branch of the Bertelsmann foundation, was founded in Barcelona with the aim of further developing the library sector in Spain, based on the Alcúdia model.

Address Fundació Biblioteca d'Alcúdia Can Torró, Carrer d'en Serra 15, 07400 Alcúdia, +34 (0)971 547311 | Getting there Bus Autocares Mallorca towards Alcúdia centre, on foot a few metres away from Plaça de la Constitució | Hours June–Sept Tue–Sun 10am–2pm, Tue–Fri 5–9pm; Oct–May Tue–Sun 10am–2pm, Tue–Fri 4–8pm | Tip In the neighbouring Can Fondo, from the 14th century, which is right next to Can Torró, there are regular exhibitions of contemporary art. The city's historical archive is also housed here.

5__ The Jakober Collection
Portraits of children in a reservoir

Everything in this art oasis is unusual, perhaps even unique. The place is quirky, the benefactors are originals, the art collection is flamboyant. The Fundación Yannick y Ben Jakober, hidden on the La Victòria peninsula and only accessible via windy roads, offers a chocolate box full of surprises, which thus far seemed to be reserved to insiders only. In fact, this cultural foundation belonging to the sculptors Yannick Vu and Ben Jakober has existed since 1993, but the collection in the Finca Sa Bassa Blanca, the 'white lagoon' – built by Egyptian architect Hassan Fathy in 1978 in a Hispanic-Moorish style – has only really gained momentum in recent years.

The portraits of aristocratic children, painted by Spanish, Flemish, English and French masters of the 16th to 19th centuries and exhibited in a former subterranean water depot, are really worth seeing. The collection contains around 150 such paintings, which also served in aristocratic circles as 'application documents' for later marriages.

Contemporary art is on show in a part of the main building, with pieces by Domenico Gnoli, Alan Rath and Meret Oppenheim. Some rooms are home to work by Rebecca Horn and Vu Cao Dam, one of the most famous Vietnamese artists of the 20th century, who lives in Paris and is Yannick Vu's father. Since 2007 there is also the Socrates hall with a very special mix of exhibits, accessible from the park via a wide staircase. Here you can see, for example, a seven-metre-wide and four-metre-high curtain by Swarovski, studded with 10,000 glittering crystals, in front of it the fossil of a roughly 120,000-year-old Siberian woolly rhinoceros alongside works by Miquel Barceló and Gerhard Merz. Noteworthy is the expansive sculpture park with numerous large animal figures made of granite by the benefactor couple themselves, who currently split their time between Costa Rica and Mallorca.

Address Museo Sa Bassa Blanca, Camí del Coll Baix, Es Mal Pas, 07400 Alcúdia, +34 (0)971 549880 or +34 (0)900 777001, www.fundacionjakober.org or www.msbb.org | Getting there Around 1.5 kilometres beyond Alcúdia you reach the district of Mal Pas. At the entrance to the town turn right at Bar Bodega des Sol into Cami de Muntanya and drive for 4 kilometres to Alcanada Golf Club and follow the sign for 'Fundacíon'. If the gate is closed, ring the bell. | Hours Mon – Sat 9.30am – 6pm; main building (only with a guided tour) daily (except Tue and Sun) 11am, noon, 3pm & 4pm | Tip The two huge granite doves on Plaça Porta de Santa Catalina in Palma are also by Ben Jakober.

6 La Victòria Hermitage

For those who'd like to sleep in a monastery

Spending the night up here, on the tip of the La Victòria peninsula, in one of the 12 monastery rooms, is like taking a trip back in time to the Middle Ages. A visit to the hermitage Petit Hotel Hostatgeria La Victòria on the Cap des Pinar with a wonderful view of the Bay of Pollença and the Cap de Formentor is also very much about inner reflection. And when the day trippers, who of course come to see the Ermita de la Victòria, under the former Carmelite monastery rooms, have left again in the evening, you are plunged into a meditative serenity that you would hardly imagine being able to find on Mallorca.

The hostel is of course monastically bare, which is why the prices are also quite modest. It is self-catering, and you have to manage with your own key after 6pm. The walls of this monastery stronghold are thick, the rooms small, the windows sometimes tiny. But the atmosphere that the house exudes can only be found here at this pilgrimage site.

The Ermita de la Victòria, which you reach at the end of a narrow winding road, is from the 13th century. There are many stories about the small church. One says that just after the Reconquista, a shepherd boy had found a statue of the Virgin Mary carved out of wood, which was then so venerated that this small chapel was built especially for it. In the 16th century the statue was stolen by pirates time and again, but miraculously it always made its way back to its original place on the altar. This is how it got its name Mare de Déu de la Victòria, Mother of God of Victory, and became a place of pilgrimage for Mallorquins. At the end of the 17th century, the church was converted and furnished with a three-part nave, a round arch and a baroque altar. At the start of the 18th century, and then again in the course of the expansion of the two floors of the hotel above it, the Ermita de la Victòria was once again restored.

Address Carrer Cap del Pinar – Ermita de la Victòria, 07400 Alcúdia, +32 (0)971 549912 |
Getting there From Alcúdia in the direction of Mal Pas or Bonaire, the road to Cap des
Pinar leads directly to Ermita de la Victòria | Hours The church is almost always open
during the daytime in summer and usually closed in winter | Tip Above the church is
Restaurant Mirador del la Victòria, from where the view is beautiful. Below it, around
800 metres away, is the small beach S'Illot.

7 — The Sant Crist Chapel

The cross of secrets

The Catholic church of Alcúdia Sant Jaume, dedicated to Saint Jacob and once part of the town's imposing defensive wall, is not the first church that has stood at this site. The original building in the south-east corner of the city is from 1248. It was replaced in the 16th century by a modern house of God, which became so dilapidated in the course of the following centuries that parts of it collapsed in 1870 and it was mainly replaced by the church that we see today, erected between 1882 and 1893 in the neo-Gothic style. But the tower and baroque Sant Crist side chapel built between 1675 and 1697 still belong to the earlier church. The impressive cross of Sant Crist, which grabs the eye as soon as you enter the chapel, visible behind the altar from afar, is approached via a stairway on the side. The coloured Christ of Alcúdia, adorned with a silver crown and face always half in shadow, is protected by a massive glass screen.

Sant Crist chapel, which was saved before the collapse of the old church, was built especially for a wooden cross and representation of Christ from the 15th century, which was thought to have performed miracles at the time and is considered to this day to have magical powers that many Mallorquins firmly believe in. So it is still a destination for many local pilgrims. In 1507, Alcúdia suffered from a devastating drought that left the people fearing a famine. In a large procession, in which they carried the cross of Sant Crist to the cave of Sant Martí in order to ask for water, the Christ of Alcúdia suddenly began to sweat blood and water, and continued to do so for three days. Thereupon it began to rain so intensely that the harvest became most bountiful.

The Alcúdia congregation has since remembered this miracle with a procession leading through the streets of the city once every three years on 26 July.

Address Plaza Jaume Qués Prevere, 07400 Alcúdia, +34 (0)971 548665 | **Getting there** Coming from Palma on the Ma-13 to Alcúdia, turn right before the city wall into Avinguda Prínzep d'Espanya, parking spaces available | **Hours** Mon–Sat 10am–1pm, Wed & Fri 5–7pm | **Tip** Diagonally opposite the church is the Museu Monogràfic de Pollèntia, Alcúdia's archaeological museum.

8 Teatre Romà

Old Rome close to the beach

In this small theatre, discovered in 1953 and then subsequently restored, on the edge of the old Roman city of Pollentia, was where the action was, with light entertainment, theatre and dance for the local population – in a typical semicircular Roman theatre with stone stands, a large stage and an orchestra platform (reserved for VIP spectators). And all this in the 1st century AD. Unlike most theatres of this kind, Teatre Romà was completely cut into the rock. Because of this, it was probably smaller than other comparable theatres of this style, with a diameter of less than 100 metres, but it nonetheless provided space for around 2,500 visitors.

Teatre Romà is part of the city of Pollentia, which was founded in 70 BC not far from the city walls of today's Alcúdia after the Romans captured Mallorca and became the capital of the Roman province of Balearica and a cultural metropolis. The structure of the old city can be seen today on the exposed ruins. The best way to discover even more details of Alcúdia's Roman past is in the Museu Monogràfic de Pollentia in Carrer Sant Jaume.

In the 5th century AD, Pollentia finally succumbed to the onslaught of the Vandals, who plundered and virtually destroyed the city. Its inhabitants fled and settled further north in today's Pollença, which they named after their old capital and where they built and left behind a series of important structures, such as the Pont Roma bridge.

The old Roman city of Pollentia itself subsequently played no further role; parts of the area and Teatre Romà were converted into burial sites for the earlier city Alcúdia.

Today's Alcúdia and also the name of the city go back to Muslim rule beginning in the 10th century. The place grew into a larger settlement with church and city wall just alongside the ruins of Pollentia only after the Reconquista in the 13th century.

Address Avinguda Prínceps d'Espanya, 07400 Alcúdia, +34 (0)971 547004,
www.pollentia.net | Getting there On foot along Cami del Teatre Romà, parallel to the
C-713 | Hours The theatre is always open. Roman city of Pollentia: Tue–Fri 10am–6pm,
Sat & Sun 10.30am–1pm; Monographic Museum: Oct–June Mon–Fri 9.30am–2.30pm,
July–Sept daily 9.30am–1.30pm | Tip In the modern cultural centre Auditori d'Alcúdia on
Plaça de la Porta de Mallorca, in front of the gates of the preserved historic city walls, there
are theatre shows, concerts and exhibitions.

9__ The Glassworks
Spanish glassblowing art with the Gordiolas

Entering the Gordiola shop on Carrer Victòria not far from the cathedral in Palma, you can sense that the very best of glassblowing awaits you in the factory near Algaida. After all, the island has a good reputation when it comes to this craft. And you're not disappointed. Coming from Palma, just before Algaida, you stumble upon the Gordiola family's factory building, built to look like a castle, which has housed a glassblowing workshop since the start of the 18th century. The young Bernado Gordiola had learned the art of glassblowing in Venice and then received a licence to operate his own glass furnace. Gordiola is one of the oldest companies of its kind on Mallorca and supplied royal families and aristocratic palaces across Europe. Around 40 years ago the family then had the factory built in the style of neo-Gothic industrial buildings. A little kitsch, but it fits in the landscape.

Glassblowing has a long tradition on Mallorca, stretching back to the time of the Phoenicians in the 2nd century BC, when they had brought their own glass furnaces with them when settling the Mallorquin coast. In the 16th and 17th centuries, well-to-do Mallorquin families imported their glass from Venice, the Mecca of international glass art. Then the Gordiolas arrived and, together with other glassblowers, were responsible for a blossoming of this art form on Mallorca. The pieces are produced according to traditional methods. In the large, open workshop hall visitors can watch the glassblowers at work, artfully forming vases, animal figures, candlesticks and other objects for daily use from hot glass. From the courtyard you can reach a small museum, which houses the Gordiola family's private collection with antique glass objects and exhibits of the most intricate stained glass. You can also buy glass items in Gordiola. They are not cheap, but they are handmade in Mallorca.

Address Carretera Palma–Mancor, 07210 Algaida, +34 (0)971 665046 | Getting there Country road from Palma to Algaida, exit at kilometre 19 | Hours Mon–Sat 9am–6pm, Sun 9.30am–1pm | Tip Gordiola has two shops in Palma, at Carrer Victòria 6 and at Jaime II. 14. In Algaida it's worth taking a look at the Sant Pere i Sant Pau church and the restored windmills.

10__ The CCA
Unusual art across a very large area

The CCA, located at the gates of Andratx at the foot of the Tramuntana mountain range, seems at first sight like a fortress, a secured fort, a Tibetan monastery behind walls, a Mexican pyramid. It is certainly a confusing piece of architecture, and if the building was standing on its own in the landscape, it would be difficult to take. But on entering the Centro Cultural Andratx, the rectangular complex by the Danish artist Jacob Asbaek gains a lightness that reconciles this initial feeling.

There are vast rooms and an infinitely large exhibition space, lots of glass and smooth exposed aggregate concrete, as well as a courtyard spanned by a bridge, a cloister surrounded by columns, a recreation of a Mallorquin monastery. The building of the roughly 4,000-square-metre CCA was initiated at the start of the 2000s by the couple Patricia and Jacob Asbeck, gallery owners from Copenhagen with a strong affinity for the island.

The idea behind it: the presentation of international contemporary, but also Mallorquin art in exhibitions that take place three or four times a year, consisting of paintings, sculptures, installations and photographs.

But the CCA also runs an artist-in-residence programme. Four spacious living and working studios are at the disposal of visual artists for free for three to six weeks, the work that they make here is then exhibited and for sale in the CCA. In the meantime, over 500 artists from more than 20 countries have been guests at the CCA. Artists can apply for a CCA residency.

The CCA, the biggest centre for contemporary art on the Balearic Islands, does not have a permanent exhibition, but rather lives from its changing displays. Furthermore it puts on regularly concerts and cultural events in the large courtyard of the 'cloister' with its water basins, which is also available to rent as a location for events.

Address Carrer Estanyera 2, 07150 Andratx, +34 (0)971 137770 | Getting there Drive from Palma on the Ma-1 to Andratx, then the Ma-10 towards Estellences, at the round-about towards Es Capdellà | Hours March–Oct Tue–Fri 10.30am–7pm, Sat & Sun 10.30am–4pm; Nov–Feb Tue–Sat 10.30am–4pm, once a month 'Meet the Artist' tour in the exhibition halls | Tip A visit to the 13th-century parish church Santa Maria is worthwhile. Modern art: a lively gallery scene has established itself in recent years in the lower old town of Palma, especially in Sant Feliu.

11 Cala Torta

With a bit of luck, a beach to yourself

This beach has been left to nature, and it should not surprise visitors to find it covered with huge amounts of washed-up seaweed, especially after heavy swells. Otherwise Cala Torta is an idyll, with far fewer random visitors than other beaches because access is quite awkward, as the bay and the beach are located at the end of a large nature reserve.

Much has changed here since summer 2019, and that's also true for the two small neighbouring bays of Cala Estreta and Cala Mitjana, which you reach through a kind of dune landscape. As cars drove up ever closer to the wild stream and thus to the beach, the entrance to the bumpy, unsurfaced Carretera de Cala Torta has been closed further up. No through road! A hanging chain blocks the way. Now, the only way to reach the beach is on foot. And the old beach kiosk, which had become very popular over many years and a trademark of the little idyll, has had to close. These were the demands of Artà town hall. To protect nature. Whether there will be a replacement is unclear, especially since the coronavirus pandemic in 2020.

But what is certain is that the picturesque bay and the beautiful, roughly 150-metre-long and 200-metre-wide natural beach with its fine white sand and bizarre rock formations will make you feel good. Those with a small parasol with them will spend a special kind of Mallorca day here. However, the slightly high lying beach that drops away relatively quickly into turquoise-coloured sea with the confluence of two fast-flowing streams, which often form a tiny 'lake', is unfortunately unsuitable for children.

If you wander right or left of Cala Torta along the coast, you will come across bunkers made by the Franco regime in the 1940s, constructed to defend against an invasion of the island by the Allies that was feared at the time.

And on a clear day you can see Menorca.

Address Carretera Cala Torta, 07579 Artà | **Getting there** From Cala Ratjada Ma-15 towards Artà, shortly before Artà turn right at the petrol station and 10 kilometres further to Cala Torta, after 7 kilometres deterioration of the road, the last 500 metres dirt track, park in good time; access to Cala Torta by coastal walk also from nearby Cala Mesquida | **Hours** Always accessible | **Tip** Between the Ma-15 and Cala Torta, not far from the beach, 1.5 kilometres away from Cala Torta is the agritourism hotel Sa Duaia, an old manor house from the 15th century. It lets simple rooms, and there is a restaurant (Carretera Cala Torta, +34 (0)651 826416).

12 The Stairs to the Lord

Lofty ascent to Santuari de Sant Salvador

The hill of Artà, visible from afar, with the old castle and the pilgrimage church of Sant Salvador, dominates this architecturally harmonious city.

Climbing the stairs, lined with crosses, up to one of the prettiest calvary hills of any Mallorquin town to Sant Salvador pilgrimage church is quite sublime. The walk up from right down in the small town with its narrow alleyways is definitely worthwhile in itself. It's certainly a bit strenuous, but a special experience, especially in the evening, when the sun begins to set and the light floods the city in gold, ochre and red. The way up the hill is signposted.

At the end of the narrow steep alleyways of Parroquia, you come across the late-Gothic fortified church Transfiguració del Senyor, built in the 16th century, which stands on the foundations of a former mosque. The way of the Cross with its 180 steps, flanked by densely growing cypresses, starts right behind the red-stone church. The path leads up to Sant Salvador, which stands where the Arabic Almudaina palace, which James I seized and moved into in 1229 after capturing the Islamic fortress, once stood.

The Sant Salvador church was finally built in 1832 in a Renaissance style and developed over the course of time into a religious centre for the citizens of Artà. The square in front of the church, which is surrounded by the fortress walls, is adorned with an impressive fountain surrounded by palm trees. Inside the church, believers especially venerate a Madonna from the 17th century, because she is believed to have saved the citizens of Artà from pirate attacks on many occasions. Other traditions date the wooden sculpture with elongated face and a baby Jesus on its lap to the 13th century. The church's two side paintings are worth a look. They show the handover of Mallorca from the Moors to King James I of Aragon and the stoning of Ramón Llull in Algeria.

Address Carrer de Castellet, 07570 Artà | **Getting there** To Artà coming from Alcúdia on the Ma-12 or from Manacor on the Ma-15. Either walk from the inner city up the steep stairs to the mount or drive by car along the outer wall to the church (signposted). There is a car park right in front of the castle walls. | **Tip** Right in front of the city is Ses Païsses, a settlement from the prehistoric Talayot culture. You can explore what you've seen more deeply in the Museu Regional d'Artà and the Plaça d'Espanya.

13__ The Women's Garden

The story of strong Mallorquin women

Two Germans involved in the feminist movement made a statement of emancipation on Mallorca many years ago, but it has remained largely unappreciated by a wider public. Perhaps also because Gabriele Schilling and Christiane von Lengerke's project was too particular. The two had created a sculpture and art garden on their finca that represents and vividly tells the stories of strong Mallorquin women through 20 designated spaces, their 'Jardí de les Dones Mallorca', the women's garden.

In 1987, the two women bought the old finca, on the way between Artà and Can Picafort, unspoiled and set back from the road, with its associated 25,000-square-metre garden, and slowly began to renovate the property. Ten years later the two friends, who were already involved in the German feminist movement, moved full-time to their finca. And then they had the idea of the women's garden. In 2016 they finally sold the finca, and went back to Germany, but fortunately the new owners agreed to the continuation of the garden.

Between the many olive, almond and carob trees they began to develop a 'path of women's history', to shine a spotlight on women who were and are largely invisible to the public. You can encounter George Sand, who, fascinated by Mallorca, endured a winter in Valldemossa at the side of Frédéric Chopin. Then there's the contemporary Mallorquin author Maria Antònia Oliver, the literature professor Carme Riera and the singer Maria del Mar Bonet. You can find the seamstress and communist activist Aurora Picornell, who was from Mallorca and was executed as a young woman in 1937, as well as Catalina Homar, the emancipated lover of Archduke Ludwig Salvator of Austria. But female Mallorquin rural workers are also represented, as well as nuns who worked on the island.

A new homage to a strong woman and her story awaits the visitor behind every almond tree.

Address Jardin de las Mujeres, Camí de Carossa kilometre 0.9, 07570 Artà,
+34 (0)672 113143, www.gartenderfrauen.com | **Getting there** Ma-12 Carretera
Artà–Can Picafort, after 1 kilometre turn off the Ma-12, then left 900 metres into
the Cami de Carossa | **Hours** Book for viewings through +34 (0)672 113143 or
anna@gartenderfrauen.com, guided tours always Wed 11am–1pm. After the tour
there's a chance for a snack. | **Tip** Ermita de Betlem is a hermitage well worth seeing
and can be reached from Artà via the winding Ma-3333.

14 The Terraces

Where the Moors left their mark on the landscape

The grapevines that were cultivated here in a major way and are now being recultivated again sporadically, were always considered superb, their wine as outstanding. And so it is no wonder that the reputation of the small mountain village on the steep slopes of the Tramuntana range also reached the Spanish mainland. Chroniclers report that at the recapture of Mallorca from Moorish rule in the 13th century, James I and his court apparently paid special attention to the wine terraces of Banyalbufar. As this is where the Malvasia grape grows and develops to full maturity, and the courts of Aragon were very fond of drinking its wine.

In this landscape, which seems almost impossible to tame, the Moors had discovered how to create a powerful terraced landscape supported by retaining walls, in order to grow vines and to farm. A sophisticated irrigation system was decisive in this. Water basins collected the sparkling water from the mountain springs and distributed it through small walled channels. The current owners of what totals over 1,000 terraces still profit from it. The name Banyalbufar also derives from the Arabic and basically means 'small vineyard by the sea'.

Banyalbufar ultimately achieved wealth and prosperity, and at the end of the 19th century was one of the richest municipalities on Mallorca. The Malvasia grape variety produced the delicious sweet dessert wines that were so popular in Palma and Barcelona. Then, around 1900, the phylloxera catastrophe broke out on the island, destroying all of the Mallorquin vineyards, including those of the small mountain village of Banyalbufar. Thousands of inhabitants of Mallorca left the island and emigrated. Mallorca only really began to recover from this disaster in the 1980s.

Today, the 600-inhabitant village is making an effort to revive the Malvasia grape on the old terraces.

Address 07191 Banyalbufar | Getting there From Palma on the Ma-1040 to Esporles, further on the Ma-1100 to the Ma-10 (Valldemossa–Andratx); Bus L 200 from Palma via Esporles | Tip Beyond Banyalbufar in the direction of Andratx on the Ma-10 you will come upon one of Mallorca's most famous lookout towers, Torre del Verger, built in the 16th century. It stands visible for miles around on the outermost edge of the cliffs and has a small viewing platform.

15 The Italian Garden

Strolling around an old palace

The country manor Raixa near Bunyola belonged to the Despuig family for over 300 years. When it was put up for sale in 2002, there were many prominent interested parties. Michael Douglas and Jil Sander both took a look at the picturesque property. Although the fashion designer offered massive sums of money for the country manor, the insular council took advantage of its right of first refusal and took over the estate including the park, with the aim of making it accessible to the public. A clever step, since Raixa had been taboo for the public for more than 30 years.

Raixa, whose origins lie in a Moorish finca from the 13th century and which, after numerous changes of owner and alterations, transferred into the ownership of the Despuig family in 1620, has a prominent son of the family clan to thank for its Italian appearance. When the cultured Antonio Despuig y Dameto (1745–1813), cardinal in Valencia, came back to Mallorca from a trip to Rome and the Holy See, he was quite convinced: Raixa should be converted into a villa based on the Italian model, with the manor house and the huge garden designed in the style of the Italian Renaissance. He was able to persuade his brother Joan, the owner of Raixa, and the work began.

The stately group of buildings around the courtyard with the central manor house and a loggia adorned by 10 column arches, the auxiliary buildings and stables, the olive press, the wine cellar and a chapel are surrounded by opulent gardens. A classical flight of stairs stands centre stage, leading to the property's very own hill with numerous terraces and structures, like an artificial grotto and a round temple from 1854 with the insignia of the Despuig family. There is also the Apollo garden and a large permanent walled carp pond with a romantic terrace. After years of elaborate renovation work, Raixa is once again open to visitors.

Address Carretera Ma-11 Palma–Sóller, 07110 Bunyola, +34 (0)971 237636 | Getting there From Palma on the Ma-11 towards Sóller, La Raixa is on the left at kilometre 12.2 before Bunyola; bus L 210, L 211 Palma–Port de Sóller, stop Bunyola or ask the driver in advance to stop at the path to Caubet (Joan March hospital) | Hours Tue–Sat 10am–3pm | Tip From Bunyola, the nearby Jardins d'Alfàbia is also worth a visit.

16 The Garden of Tolerance
The art of Dörte Wehmeyer

The glazed main building of the futuristic looking Can Blau finca, with the pool further down towards the cliffs and its views of the far-off island of Cabrera, are already extravagant and architecturally eccentric. The property's vast gardens, the studio and the exhibition space are elusive. The garden of tolerance by the installation artist Dörte Wehmeyer, who is originally from Cologne, is not easy viewing, but rich in insight and worth seeing. The artist opens her garden to the public twice a year, but you can also arrange a spontaneous visit at any other time, and immerse yourself in this art landscape and let the powerful sculptures of iron, glass, stone, coal, mirrors and paper take their effect.

You enter a labyrinth of welded steel walls, floating windows and mirrors, encounter chair formations that reach up towards the sky, a huge cross with books integrated in it, a reproachful and warning sign claiming the 'banality of evil', a wherry full of shattered glass stranded by some water, a staircase leading into nothingness, burnt books. Then there are the installations in a 400-square-metre underground studio, accessible via folding stairs, under a water basin. Here the visitor is confronted with everyday objects detached from their intended use, arranged in surprising contexts, highlighted by visual effects, both meaningful and evocative. The artist, who has twice been invited to the Venice Biennale in past years and is heavily influenced by the Arte Povera, 'land art' and 'social sculpture' of Joseph Beuys, processes the horrors of the past and the injustices of the present in her art: from German fascism and Islamic terror to the harassment of indigenous peoples, refugee dramas and the climate crisis.

The garden of tolerance contains her permanent exhibition on the theme of 'violence and humanity', which she has continued to develop over the years.

Address Can Blau, Carrer de la Fontanella 7, 07690 Cala Llombards-Santanyí, www.doertewehmeyer.com | Getting there From Santanyí on the Ma-6100 towards Es Llombards to the roundabout, then turn half left, after 800 metres turn into Camí de Cala Llombards and drive to the end of the road | Hours On open days, private views or by appointment with the artist at doertewehmeyer@gmail.com; organised guided tours via Ingrid Flohr, +34 (0)690 218709, www.kunst-touren-mallorca.com | Tip The fine sandy beaches and steep shores of Cala Santanyí and Cala Llombards invite you to swim and relax.

17 __ Castell de n'Amer
Strategic point on the east coast

The Mallorquins have had quite a cross to bear over the centuries with pirates: raids, pillaging, destruction over and over again. And these seafaring gangs were very hard to control. After their raids, the pirates would quickly retreat back to the other Balearic Islands or for example to Cabrera just off Mallorca. The pirate ships also frequently found cover and refuge in one of the many bays on the island's rugged coast. The pirates developed, no matter who happened to rule Mallorca, into a permanent threat. After Ottoman pirates had plundered and almost completely destroyed the villages of Andratx, Sóller, Alcúdia and Pollença in the course of the Turkish invasion of the Mediterranean from 1550 to 1553, the systematic construction of watch towers along the coast began one by one. Over 80 such towers were ultimately built into a fortification network.

This included the castle-like defence tower Castell de n'Amer on Punta de n'Amer peninsula on the east coast of Mallorca between Cala Millor and Sa Coma, a nature conservation area covered in dunes and small pine forests. However, Castell de n'Amer, although long planned, was first realised over 100 years later in 1696 after repeated attacks by north African pirates. It is surrounded by a deep trench and is accessed over a drawbridge. A narrow stone spiral staircase leads up to the upper cannon platform with an old cannon. It served the Francoists as an observation tower in the Spanish Civil War from 1936 to 1939 and was fiercely contested during the landing of Republican troops on the peninsula in the 'Battle of Mallorca' in 1936, and was in their hands for some time. There is now a small museum inside the Castell with old weapons, uniforms, artefacts used in the fortress and documents, as well as a plan of the defence and lookout towers along the coast. There are some spectacular views from the top.

Address 07530 Cala Millor | **Getting there** By foot or bike, and also by car if it's not busy. To be reached from Sa Coma (1.5 kilometres) from end of the north beach promenade or from Cala Millor (1.3 kilometres) from the southern end (signposted). The peninsula is privately owned, but freely accessible. | **Hours** Open during the day, and can be viewed for free | **Tip** There is a small restaurant with the best views in some outbuildings that once belonged to the Castell.

18 Casa March Park

The richest man on the island once resided here

One of Mallorca's most glamorous private houses opens out visible from afar high up on the mountain above the port of Cala Ratjada. Casa March, the home of the most powerful family that ever called the shots on Mallorca, deciding the island's fate over decades in all respects.

Casa March was the residence of Juan March and his entourage, alongside an opulent city villa in Palma and numerous other properties and estates on the island, set in a spacious park landscape. The godfather of Mallorca, who had accumulated his fortune through the most shady of tricks, a banking empire, shipping companies and hotel complexes, was the boss here. But in order for future generations to put it in a positive light, the March dynasty decided to rededicate their Casa as an event location of the exalted muse alongside an openly accessible park, rich in cultural treasures. The property now belongs to the Fundación Bartolomé March, but is still privately owned by the family.

In 1915, Juan March had this opulent summer residence built on the ruins of a 15th-century watch tower, architecturally ingenious and furnished inside with mosaics and murals. In the 1960s, the March family had the 60-hectare park around the Villa Sa Torre Cega ('the blind tower') lavishly designed by the renowned English landscape architect Russell Page and developed into a sculpture garden with dozens of works by Auguste Rodin, Henry Moore and Eduardo Chillida. In the building itself there were works by Picasso and Goya, but also contemporary work. In 2001, an apocalypse came down over Casa March. A hurricane devastated the high-altitude March garden, ripped out trees, destroyed the irrigation system and demolished numerous sculptures. The park had to be closed. The garden was first reopened in its original condition, in the presence of the Spanish king, in mid-2011.

Address Sa Torre Cega, Carrer Juan March 2, 07590 Cala Ratjada, +34 (0)971 711122 |
Getting there Buses from Palma, Artà, Can Picafort and Cala Millor to Cala Ratjada
(Carrer Castellet) several times a day; by car on the Ma-15 via Capdepera. | **Hours**
May–Nov Wed–Fri 10.30am–noon, Sat & Sun 11am–6pm; Feb–Apr Wed & Sat
11am–12.30pm, Fri 11am–2pm; reservation necessary, guide tour included in price,
+34 (0)689 027353 | **Tip** There are two pretty and quiet sandy beaches, largely left to
nature with dune landscape and trees, worth a visit not far from Cala Ratjada: Cala Agulla
and Cala Mesquida. Nearby Torre Embucada with its lighthouse forms the most easterly
point on Mallorca.

19 __ The Rock Arch

An object of art created by nature

Most Mallorca holidaymakers think they know the rock arch near the fine sand of Cala Santanyí. This is because they have seen it so often on photos that they've begun to believe that they've actually witnessed it in reality. A self-deception – the gigantic rock gateway off the cliffs near Cala Santanyí is not easy to find and hard to reach. You really have to be looking for this unique place, on the steep slope, in strong winds. You can also reach it along the cliffs beyond the Bay of Cala Santanyí, sheltered from the wind by the surrounding high rocks and planted with pines, towards the picturesque Cala Llombards.

The rock 'Es Pontas' is a natural wonder that will take your breath away when you come face to face with it. The stone gateway, that rises up out of the sea, can never be conveyed so powerfully in a photo. A massive rock formation towers up from the blue water into a huge bridge, free standing and ending in the sea on both sides. This rock has been flushed out by the water over millions of years. Many also call Es Pontas 'Mallorca's gate to the sea'. It goes without saying that this spectacular natural wonder is especially popular among divers and extreme climbers.

There are numerous extreme rock formations, spectacular crevices and rock holes on the island, that are like natural works of art. In Cala de Sa Comuna you can, for example, jump into the sea through a hole in the rock. Right in front of the rock bridge Es Pontas one encounters a piece of art that is from a more recent period, but which seems no less archaic. The artist Rolf Schaffner piled up nine massive blocks of rock into a six-metre-high object, whose counterparts, according to the artist, are to be found in cruciform, starting from Cologne in Germany, to Trondheim in Norway, Volgograd in Russia and Cork in Ireland. The name of the object ensemble: *Equilibrio* (equilibrium).

Address 07650 Cala Santanyí | Getting there From Santanyí on the Ma-6102, right just before Cala Santanyí up towards Hotel Pinos Playa and park, walk to the cliffs and lookout point | Tip A similar natural wonder is the rocky headland Na Foradada with an 18-metre hole in the rock wall (Mirador de na Foradada, Ma-10 from Valldemossa to Deìa at kilometre 65).

20__ The Church Painting
Bartolomé Murillo in the side chapel

Sant Julià parish church in Campos, built between 1858 and 1873 in a neo-classical style on the foundations of a church from the 15th century, sneaks under every tourist radar. But the almost 50-metre-long and 25-metre-tall nave, when it's open and also well-lit, will have you under its spell from the moment you enter. The round arched vault with its immense blue-white coffered ceiling, which, like a firmament, is made up of 817 gilded panels, is outstanding. You won't find anything like this anywhere else on the island. Then there's the Gothic altar picture by the Mallorquin painter and sculptor Gabriel Móger (1379–1439) from the previous church, of which the bell tower is still standing, with its figure of Saint Julian, the patron saint of Campos, on the spire. The church, the third at this location, stands out particularly through its 12 side chapels with numerous significant exhibits.

But the most important picture in terms of art and church history stands behind a large, wrought-iron grille in the side chapel to the right of the altar: *Santa Cristo de la Paciencia* by the painter Bartolomé Esteban Murillo (1618–1682) from Seville, whose pictures achieved top prices at auction in the 19th century. He was, alongside Diego Velázquez, one of the most famous representatives of Spanish baroque painting in the 17th century. This painting, one of Murillo's religious images from around 1640, shows Jesus before the beginning of the Passion, under olive trees in the garden of Gethsemane. Alone, in the midst of his sleeping disciples. Before the interrogation by the high priests Annas and Kaiphas, knowing what awaits him, yet calm in inner humility.

The unusual picture was bought in 1798 by Julià Ballester from Campos on the orders of his employer Cardinal Antoni Despuig, and brought from Seville to Mallorca, where it has been on view ever since.

Address Església Sant Julià, Carrer Bisbe Talladas 17, 07630 Campos, +34 (0)971 650003 | Getting there On the Ma-19 to Campos | Hours Sat 10am–1pm, out of service times collect the key at Casa Rectoria 17 opposite, museum in the sacristy by appointment on +34 (0)971 650003 | Tip In Campos, Torre des Cancos, a square defence tower from the 17th century, is worth seeing. The bakery Pomar is also recommended (Carrer Plaça, 20).

21 The Saltworks
Flor de Sal d'Es Trenc as top brand

You would hardly believe how many different types of salt there are. And among the best are those from Mallorca; more precisely from the saltworks at Es Trenc. The idea of developing this salt beyond the status of a normal table salt came from a young Swiss businesswoman at the start of 2000. She secured access to the saltworks between Colònia de Sant Jordi and the dune beach Es Trenc and made Flor de Sal into a successful brand – with a small shop at the saltworks and a shop in Santanyí. The factory owned by the small company, for which around 10 people work, was also very close by. In 2017, the Swiss entrepreneur sold her lucrative business. Today, the products are on offer in numerous European countries, including Great Britain.

Flor de Sal d'Es Trenc is an absolutely natural product with a particularly high mineral and magnesium content, but also an exceptional taste. The prerequisites: crystal clear seawater and a constant breeze. When sun and air make the water collected in the salt pans evaporate, the snow-white salt is left behind, crystallised. The upper layer of these fine salt crystals is skimmed off by hand with special hooks, 'harvested' and dried. There is Flor de Sal as pure sea salt, or refined in Santanyí with Mallorquin herbs and spices, which then yield very special flavours.

Salt production has been a part of Mallorquin life from time immemorial. The Phoenicians made their salt in the nearby saltworks of Llevant, just like the Romans and the Arabs who followed. There has been a brisk trade in salt since the 13th century. Salt has been harvested at the saltworks of Es Trenc since the middle of the last century. In the meantime, Flor de Sal from Es Trenc has developed into a real hit. It is sold in delicatessen shops and is greeted with keen interest not only among gourmet chefs, but also from evermore private gourmets.

Address Salines d'Es Trenc (Shop), Carretera Campos–Colonia Sant Jordi, 07630 Campos, +34 (0)971 655629 | Getting there Carretera Ma-6040 Campos–Colonia Sant Jordi, kilometre 8.7, then right into the side street Es Trenc, continue to the car park by the beach | Hours Shop in the saltworks daily 10am–7.30pm, guided tours daily from 10am up to six times a day, +34 (0)971 655629 | Tip There are also Flor de Sal shops in Ses Salines, Artà, Alcúdia and Pollença or online at www.flordesaldestrenc.com.

22 Graffiti

Street art between hotel blocks

In the last three years, Can Picafort has become a stronghold for graffiti and street art. What was once the illegal spraying and painting of dreary façades is now seen as a legal enhancement of a hotel resort along the coast that is not exactly architecturally endowed. An enterprising city council and the creative know-how of young graffiti artists have given the beach resort a new image, that is also positively appreciated by most guests.

Today, Can Picafort has a new side and a bright new light in which to show itself.

One of the stars of the scene is Joan Aguiló from Palma, who studied graphic design and art in his home town and Barcelona. He is one of the initiators of the annual Saladina Art Festival in Can Picafort, which has taken place annually since 2016, where art in public space is the focus, with national and international street artists. Figurative painting, often close to photorealism, dominates. Here are huge beach and bathing scenes on the dreary and monotonous house walls of hotels and apartment blocks, scenes from the life of the holiday and beach resort. Gigantic eye-catchers, but also small intricate works of art on benches and the corners of houses. A colourful styling of public space, that turns a stroll into an art experience.

You'll come across 10-metre-tall towers time and again in and around Can Picafort, and also right at the harbour exit. These structures, that stand like obelisks at 1,240-metre intervals along the beaches, each have a counterpart around 200 metres inland. A twin tower. All of the towers between Port d'Alcúdia and Colònia de Sant Pere, most of them white with a red tip visible from afar, served submarine captains in the Spanish Civil War and later in World War II as orientation points. The Puntos de Referencia were also fixed points for the Spanish navy for target practice during simulated land invasions, a threat that seemed real for decades.

Address Promenade and adjacent roads, 07458 Can Picafort | Getting there Carretera Ma-12 Alcúdia–Artà, Can Picafort, into Carrer Mar to the harbour and to the promenade | Hours Always accessible | Tip The number of large-scale works of graffiti in Palma has skyrocketed in recent years, especially in the old town. A garish and colourful over-sized graffito that shows all kinds of international pop stars, painted over and beyond part of a house wall, is worth seeing (corner of Carrer de Cotoner and Carrer de Bayarte).

23 __ The Sculptures
Joan Bennàssar on the beach

The sculptures, between 1.5 and 3 metres tall, stand in exposed locations. Not directly in the sand, but perhaps slightly washed around by the water or on protruding rocks, one right by the harbour, then again close to the nearby bunker. They are distributed in four groups, formed of cement, and firmly anchored to the ground. Female figures, goddesses perhaps, fairies or some kind of fairytale characters, always voluptuous and naked.

They stand there within sight and calling range of hundreds of holidaymakers enjoying themselves on the beach here. It's to be expected that selfies are taken and photos shot with the buxom figures, even if only to document the takers' own suntans and slimness. At the end of the season, peace returns to the beach and promenade, and the sculptures appear in another light.

The groups of figures are called *El Deseo* (desire), *El Ritual*, (ritual) *El Tesoro* (treasures) or *La Herida* (the wound) and are all by the internationally renowned draughtsman, painter, sculptor and ceramicist Joan Bennàssar. Born in 1950 in Pollença, where he also lived and worked, the artist created the permanent sculpture exhibition *Puertos de Alga Marina* ('ports of seaweed') on the promenade and beach of Can Picafort, which lend the tourist town, crowded in summer, but virtually deserted in autumn and winter, an extravagant note.

Joan Bennàssar, who attended the academies in Palma and Barcelona, describes his art as 'Mediterranean'. The charm of the sea plays a dominant role in his work. He calls himself a 'primitivist', heavily inspired by Francis Bacon and Pablo Picasso. He loves to create allegorical figures of island history that are metaphors. The artist, who belongs to the influential generation of Spanish painters such as Miquel Barceló, Ramón Canet or José María Sicilia, has imposing works of art in numerous places on Mallorca.

Address Promenade and beach: Carrer Cervantes, Carrer Enginyer Felicià Fuster and Carrer Marina, 07458 Can Picafort | Getting there Carretera Ma-12 Alcúdia–Artà, Can Picafort, onto Carrer Mar to the harbour and the promenade | Hours Always accessible | Tip Beyond the district of Son Bauló, on the edge of a dune landscape, you will come across the prehistoric burial site Necròpolis de Son Real, with over 100 graves enclosed by walls.

24 The Southern Tip
Untouched nature around the lighthouse

The southernmost point of the island can confidently be described as rustic. There is no bus service, tour buses rarely stray here, and you don't see many cars either. Those who drive through or wander around this piece of almost untouched landscape are mainly the kind of people who like peace and quiet and who really want to escape the turmoil of the beaches. Apart from landscape and nature there is nothing really of note – and no restaurants or cafés. When conditions are good, you can see out to the island of Cabrera, and of course there is the white lighthouse with its elongated keeper's house, which marks the southern end of Mallorca and is a real attraction, not only for lighthouse fetishists. But it is often stormy here on the Cap; metre-high waves lash against the rocky coast, spray exploding in all directions.

On the journey to Cap de ses Salines you pass by the salt flats of Sa Vall, which alongside those of Colònia Sant Jordi are among the oldest on the island, and were already used for salt production through the evaporation of sea water in Roman times. But the overwhelming majority of Mallorca's southern tip belongs to the March banking family, so it is private property, and the estates such as the S'Avall estate are mostly fenced in. But that shouldn't spoil your enjoyment.

From the lighthouse you can wander on the coast, when the weather is good, preferably in the direction of Colònia de Sant Jordi always along the cliffs. The many species of birds you encounter here are especially fascinating. Alongside the native birds, thousands of migratory birds land here on their way from Africa to their breeding grounds in Europe. If you walk for a good half hour, through rough terrain it must be said, you will come across the Platja des Caragol, a real piece of seclusion, far away from any tourism, as this beach can only be reached on foot.

Address Cap de ses Salines (belongs to the municipality 07650 Santanyí) | Getting there From Palma on the Ma-19 to Llucmajor, Campos and Santanyí, from there or from Ses Salines on the Ma-6100 and Ma-6110 to the lighthouse on Cap de ses Salines | Tip In Ses Salines you should take a look at the Sant Bartomeu church and the remains of the 13th-century Torre de Can Bárbara fortress.

25 The Battlements

The splendid castle protects a saint and vice versa

You should definitely scale Mallorca's largest fortress by foot. The steep stairs, with 150 steps, lead up from the centre of the town. What awaits you there, high above the roofs of Capdepera, is certainly worth the climb. A restored fortress, where the townspeople once found refuge from advancing pirates, and another view, to be enjoyed preferably in the evening towards sunset.

The mountain has always attracted people. The Romans settled up here to control the plains. The Moors expanded the complex further, building the Miquel Nunis tower, which is still standing today but converted in the meantime into a mill, between the 10th and 12th century. After the Moors had long been conquered in Palma, they were still stubbornly resisting the troops of James I of Aragón and the Reconquista in Capdepera in 1230. James II had the fortress expanded in around 1300, and the local population lived within the walls in small houses to protect themselves from pirate attacks. Castell de Capdepera was thought for a long time to be impregnable, and kept its function as a fortified village up until the 18th century. With the enlargement of the town and a new city wall built lower down, the fort lost its function and became derelict. The restoration only began in 1983.

Within the accessible castle walls, completely equipped with battlements, you can still see the Arabic tower, the house of the governor, which now contains a museum about the art of palm leaf weaving cultivated in Capdepera, and the late-Gothic chapel of Nuestra Senyora de la Esperança from the 14th century. 'Our Lady of Hope', venerated to this day, is supposed to have protected Capdepera time and again from pirate attacks. It is believed that when she was placed on the battlements, thick fog drew in, which made the pirates retreat. The delicate Madonna is the patron saint of Capdepera to this day.

Address Carrer Castell de Capdepera, 07580 Capdepera, +34 (0)971 818746 | Getting there From Palma on the Ma-15 via Manacor and Artà | Hours 16 Mar–14 Oct daily 9am–8pm, 15 Oct–15 Mar daily 9am–5pm | Tip Those who are courageous and do not shy away from taking the more difficult path, can set off on another tour through the magnificent landscape of the Parc Natural Peninsula del Llevant armed with a good map.

26__The Caves
Journey to the Centre of the Earth

In the Coves d'Artà – unlike most caves on Mallorca, which are often warm and humid and sweaty, and often require you to stoop in order to advance – magnificent stalactite chambers open up, huge halls with unparalleled large stalagmites, arcades of chalk formations, all at a constant temperature of around 18 degrees. Wandering upright through this cave labyrinth is like a visit to a museum.

The cave, which has belonged to the municipality of Capdepera since 1858 – its name comes from the time when this region was still part of Artà – is on Cap Vermell around 50 metres above the sea on the picturesque cliffs of the Bay of Canyamel. The Coves d'Artà is thought to have been created millions of years ago, when the massif imploded. The cave was already known to Mallorca's indigenous people. In 1229, Moorish warriors fled from an approaching band of James I's soldiers into the catacombs, and pirates hoarded their loot here time and again.

It was opened to the public in 1806. The labyrinth caves were entered bearing torches and became one of the island's oldest tourist attractions. The author Jules Verne is supposed to have found his inspiration for the novel *Journey to the Centre of the Earth* here.

No wonder. The 75-metre-long and up to 25-metre-high 'Vestibule' is already captivating. In its dome hang hundreds of intricate and bizarre stalactites. Slim, mysterious ghost-like stalagmites rise up from the ground.

Through a column chamber with thousands of the most curious stalactite formations, reminiscent of Gothic architecture, one reaches the oval 'Hall of the Queen of Columns', in the middle of which a 22-metre-tall and six-million-year-old column, the tallest stalagmite in Europe, dominates. Ghostly wall reliefs, highlighted by a spectacular illumination, await in the gigantic 'Hell' and finally in the cathedral-like 'Glory'.

Address Coves d'Artà, Carretera de las Cuevas, 07580 Capdepera, +34 (0)971 841293 | **Getting there** Coming from Artà on the Ma-4042 towards Canyamel, turn left before Torre de Canyamel, past the golf course to the coast, from the car park to the cave on foot | **Hours** Apr, May, June, Oct 10am–6pm; July, Aug, Sept 10am–7pm, Nov–Mar 10am–5pm, only as part of a guided tour, multilingual | **Tip** Another underground cave worth seeing is in Campanet. Nearby on the surface you can witness the karstic spring phenomena of Ses Fonts Ufanes: between November and April, when the rain is strong, water begins to bubble up from numerous springs in the ground of the holm oak forest.

27 The Torre

The defence tower of Canyamel

This mighty tower is not a replica based on medieval ruins, like so many, often quite tacky specimens you will come across on the island, but rather a former escape and defence tower dating back to the 13th century. This building, unique in the form on the island and named Torre d'en Montsó after the prosperous founding family in the 15th century, was part of the defence system against enemies, especially pirates, who constantly threatened the island and the coast and troubled the valley of Canyamel time and again. But the tower also symbolised the wealth of the Mallorquin estates located in this fertile area, which ran very lucrative sugar cane growing businesses, especially in the 15th century.

The Torre de Canyamel (sugar cane tower), roughly four kilometres away from Capdepera, with its surrounding farm buildings and the old oil mill, which now houses the Porxada de Sa Torre restaurant, which opened in summer 2006 – specialities are the traditional 'Terrina' (stew) and the 'Porcella' (suckling pig) – measures almost 25 metres tall on a quadratic floor plan. From far away, the three-storey building looks like the relic of a gigantic film set. With its crenellations and roof terrace surrounded by battlements and a five-metre-tall lookout tower with views to the coast on top, it is thought to stand on Moorish foundations. It is said that the tower from the time of Spanish King James I, which forms a line with the fortifications of Torre Miquel Nunis and Castells Capdepera, never fell into enemy hands, in spite of numerous pirate attacks.

Today, the former farm buildings that surround the Torre house a private museum, with an exhibition of typical local rural instruments of the past. In the tower itself, which can also be viewed by appointment, there are numerous summer exhibitions and concerts in a very special, very delightful atmosphere.

Address Torre de Canyamel, Carretera Artà, Carretera de Canyamel, 07580 Capdepera, +34 (0)971 841134 | Getting there On the Ma-4040 between Servera and Capdepera to the junction to the Ma-4042 from Artà, then to the coast towards Coves d'Artà | Hours Museum and tower: Apr–end Oct Tue–Sat 10am–3pm & 5–8pm, Sun 10am–3pm; Restaurant: Apr–end Oct daily except Mon 1–3.30pm & 7–11pm | Tip A visit to the Centre Melis Cursach, a former pharmacy, which is now a museum and exhibition hall, in Capdepera is worthwhile (Carrer des Centre 9, +34 (0)971 556479, Tue–Sun 10am–9pm, Wed 10am–1pm).

28 __ The Talayot Settlement
The prehistoric, to marvel at and touch

Capocorb Vell is probably Mallorca's most significant prehistoric settlement, certainly the best preserved, even though the Christian Reconquistas under King James I had, in their rage against anything alien, parts of the old Talayot settlement and the walls that surrounded them torn down in the 13th century. The large stone blocks were unceremoniously carted off for the building of new churches, especially the cathedral in Palma.

However, there is still much to see in Capocorb Vell today. The ruins are most likely from the 12th century BC and are thus the oldest traces of a settlement on Mallorca. The Talayot culture or Bronze Age lasted from 1400 to 1000 BC. Built in the megalithic form, using the dry wall construction method, in which stone is hewn into an angular form and only layered and interlaid, around 500 people probably lived here, not far from Llucmajor. Megalithic structures, which were common on the Balearics up until the Roman era, can be found all around the Mediterranean.

Today we can see, on a exposed area of around 7,000 square metres, three relatively well-preserved Talayots, round fortified towers, up to six metres tall with extremely thick walls, two quadratic Talayots, some with two storeys and stone floors, and two dozen residential units, surrounded by the remains of a defensive wall. It is presumed that Capocorb Vell was inhabited by people from the Bronze Age up until the early Middle Ages. However, archaeologists have no definitive answers to the question as to what the Talayot culture and these structures were really about. Were they purely defensive installations, sacrificial sites or predominantly living spaces? There are thought to have been up to 200 such villages on Mallorca. Alongside Capocorp Vell, the settlements of Ses Païsses near Artà, Necrópolis near Can Picafort and Son Fornés near Montuiri are still preserved today.

Address Poblado talayótico de Capocorb Vell, 07620 Llucmajor, +34 (0)971 180155 |
Getting there Ma-19 Palma towards Llucmajor, exit at kilometre 26, Ma-6015 towards
S'Estanyol, turn onto the Ma-6014 at kilometre 11 towards Cala Pi to kilometre 23 | **Hours**
Daily except Thu 10am–5pm | **Tip** The Museum Arqueológico Son Fornés in Montuïri
gives vivid insight into the Talayot culture and megalithic structures.

29 — The Artist's Finca

Sculpture garden in Llevant

Behind a thick hedge at the end of the expansive art garden, full of sculptures and installations, is the workshop of the sculptor Rudi Neuland. And there you can see a huge vice, different sized hammers and chisels, a chainsaw, a welding machine, mills, tree trunks, lumps of rock, metal sheets. This is where the objects of bronze, steel, wood, stone and concrete, which can be admired in the spacious garden, but also in the finca's studio, are created.

The former businessman, who found his way to sculpture as an autodidact 25 years ago and has made his one-time hobby into his profession, presents his works, around 100 different sculptures, in the Mediterranean ambience of his finca's sculpture garden between cypresses, agaves and olive trees. The works of the sculptor, who lived for many years in Cape Town, South Africa and still has his bronze sculptures cast there, are strongly influenced by life and art on the Cape and by the ambience of the townships. Rudi Neuland deals with the real and abstract, sometimes mercilessly with the sensitivities of people, showing their charm and eroticism, but also their inner conflict and vulnerability. Numerous sculptures were created in South Africa and shipped to Mallorca.

Over the years, Neuland and his wife, the gallery owner Anna Will, have made an art oasis from the 120-year-old finca in southeast Mallorca. Alongside the sculpture garden and the gallery, there is also a music room, in which piano evenings regularly take place, with acclaimed young pianists, all of them award winners of international music competitions.

During their stay on Mallorca, the musicians live in the guesthouse of the Finca Can Brut. Rudi Neuland and Anna Will have decided to open up their finca to friends of art and culture, for openings, concerts and readings. The cultural programme is organised by the gallery owner Ingrid Flohr.

Address Finca Can Brut, 07208 Cas Concos, www.rudi-neuland.de | **Getting there**
From Felanitx on the Ma-14 towards Santanyí, after Cas Concos at the left bend in the
Ma-14 drive straight on, after around 1.5 kilometres on your left | **Hours** By appointment
through +34 (0)971 839691 or RN@rudi-neuland.de or anna@piano-and-art.de or Ingrid
Flohr, Arte y Cultura, +34 (0)690 218709, www.galeriaflohr@gmx.net | **Tip** Meet at Café
Sublims on Porta Murada in Santanyí or enjoy a drink in Sa Cova, the bar owned by
German actor Uwe Ochsenknecht, on Plaça Major.

30__ The Cabrera Centre

An archipelago with many facets

Romantics associate the island of Cabrera, off the coast of the southernmost part of Mallorca, with a piece of almost untouched nature. For historians it is the old merciless prison island, which became the 'hell of Cabrera' at the start of the 19th century. The Peninsular War of independence (1808–1814) was raging when Spain struck back against the Napoleonic troops, who were grasping for control of the Iberian peninsula. When the Spanish were able to inflict a damning defeat on the French in the Battle of Bailén in 1808, taking close to 18,000 prisoners, they shipped around 9,000 of them in inhumane conditions to the almost uninhabited island of Cabrera and abandoned them there. They interned them in the old fortress, which was built in the 14th century as a defence against pirates and smugglers.

The soldiers were largely left to look after themselves, forgotten by the rest of the world. There was hardly any food, insufficient water and no medical care. Around 6,000 Frenchmen died in an agony of starvation, illness and epidemics during this six-year imprisonment. Inscriptions on the walls of the fortress still provide silent witness to the human dramas of these years.

The Cabrera archipelago, with its 17 small rocky islets and the main island, almost 14 kilometres from the coast, is also largely unknown to most Mallorquins. However, the centuries-old military fort and barrack island was proclaimed a national park in 1991. There are only a few houses and military barracks and a handful of inhabitants on Cabrera. But the diversity of wildlife on this archipelago makes it worth a visit. However, no more than 200 visitors are allowed to land on the island in a day.

The Cabrera visitors' centre in Colònia de Sant Jordi, which opened in 2008, is a building that was architecturally inspired by a Talayot, and is well worth seeing.

Address Visitors' centre of the Cabrera national park, Carrer Gabriel Roca 20, 07638 Colònia de Sant Jordi, +34 (0)971 656282 | Getting there By boat from Colònia de Sant Jordi from Apr to Oct daily (except at rough seas) around 9.30am, return around 5pm. Journey time one hour. Take food with you, as there are no restaurants. You are not allowed to visit the island on your own initiative. Bookings for ferryboats at the harbour, +34 (0)971 649034. | Hours June–Sept daily 10am–7pm, Oct, Nov, Feb–Apr 10am–2pm & 3–6pm | Tip A visit to the Blue Grotto Sa Cova Blava in Cabrera, which is only accessible from the sea, is a must. Unbelievable light reflections, swimming is allowed and it is a real experience.

31__ The Carrara Temple

The Austrian Archduke meditated in Son Marroig

What an estate, this Son Marroig, what an unparalleled, privileged location. And what a quirky owner this Archduke Ludwig Salvator of Austria (1847–1915) must have been. He had this old fortified finca with the fortress tower high above the Costa Nord remodelled in an Italian style and filled it with the life that you can still sense today when you enter and wander through it, even though it has been a museum since 1928.

You can almost see this liberally nurtured, scientifically educated, materially independent maverick and dropout from the norms of the imperial Vienna court in front of you, sitting under the round roof of the small pavilion made of Italian Carrara marble, built in a style based on antiquity, and getting high on the view. With friends, guests and lovers and twice also with his cousin, Empress Elisabeth, Sisi, who visited him here. The wide-open sea, the enchanted path down to the bay, in which his motorised sailing yacht *Nixe* was moored, with which he explored the furthest corners of the Mediterranean, the rocky headland Na Foradada with the 18-metre hole in the rock wall that lies 250 metres below the property, like a wonder of nature.

The Archduke had bought land from the farmers on a kilometre-long swathe stretching along the coast between Valldemossa and Deià and deep inland. He bought the Son Marroig property, alongside the old derelict Miramar monastery, in 1872 and lived there after its conversion until 1913. He had paths laid out and viewpoints built that were accessible to everyone. On his estates he forbade the felling of trees and any kind of hunting. Ludwig Salvator was a patron of the most genteel kind. He spoke fluent Mallorquin, was always close to the people and is revered on the island to this day, writing numerous books, including several volumes of *The Balearic Islands, portrayed in words and images*.

Address Carretera Valldemossa–Sóller, 07179 Deià, +34 (0)971 639158 | **Getting there** Ma-10 between Deià and Valldemossa, junction kilometre 65.5 to the car park; bus L 210 from Palma via Valldemossa | **Hours** Mon–Sat 9.30am–2pm & 3–5.30pm | **Tip** Not far off is the Monestir de Miramar monastery with its pretty cloister, built in 1276 by King James II and restored by the Archduke in 1872.

32_Graves' Grave

Robert Graves rests high up on the mountain

From the 1920s on, the mountain village of Deià, in the Tramuntana range, was a real artists' oasis. Painters, musicians and especially writers settled here, inspired by the beauty of the landscape, the mild climate and the flair of the place with the nearby Cala Deià. This image held right into the 1980s; artist meetings and the wild parties in the houses and bars of Deià were legendary. Deià has still preserved much of this atmosphere to this day. The village is unspoilt, original, but a little more chic, and of course there are not quite so many artists living there now. But Deià in no way lives purely on the past, when authors such as Jakov Lind and Robert Graves set the tone here. It was Robert Graves (1895–1985), who had lived here since the 1940s, in particular that shaped this little village and made it well known around the world.

So it is that the author of the novel *I, Claudius* was also buried in the small cemetery next to the Sant Joan parish church high up on the mountain, which can be reached through narrow alleyways. His house Ca n'Alluny, where he lived for half a century, became a museum in 2006 and gives an insight into the author's life and work.

It was the international fame of Robert Graves that attracted evermore artists to Deià. He invited writers and painters to stay with him, many of whom stayed on. In the 1960s and 1970s, numerous Bohemians and hippies joined them, the picturesque village with its olive terraces and citrus fruit below the 1,000-plus-metre-tall Teix mountain became evermore colourful and creative. Ava Gardner lived here, Peter Ustinov, Georg Stefan Troller, Andrew Lloyd Webber. Deià still cultivates the image of the artists' colony today, and there are still artists, who work, exhibit, sell and live here, although a rather more wealthy new clientele increasingly dominates the small village.

Address Plaça des Puig, 07179 Deià | **Getting there** Ma-10 coming from Sóller or Valldemossa; bus L 210 Palma–Valldemossa–Deià–Sóller | **Hours** Museum La Casa de Robert Graves, +34 (0)971 636185, www.lacasaderobertgraves.org: Apr–Oct Mon–Fri 10am–5pm, Sat 10am–3pm; Nov–Mar Mon–Fri 9am–4pm, Sat 9am–2pm | **Tip** It's worth taking a look at the tiny hamlet of Lluc Alcari a few kilometres beyond Deià in the direction of Sóller. Cala de Deià is one of the prettiest bays for swimming along the Tramuntana coast.

33 The Donkey
Unusual art in Tramuntana

There is something poignant about standing in front of the metal donkey by the artist Mariano Navares in Estellencs and at the same time hearing the sound of several donkeys and mules calling or braying coming up from the valley and down from the mountains. The extraordinary sculpture at the entrance to the 350-resident village Estellencs is called *Mulus Ferreus*, and stopping to look at it is *de rigueur* for every visitor. It is a homage to the animal that is still ubiquitous here, and was the only form of transport in this remote area for hundreds of years, connecting the small community with the outside world.

Estellencs is a tiny, sleepy village, which can only be reached on the winding, spectacular coastal road Ma-10 from Andratx or Valldemossa, far from mass tourism, high over the nearby coast and below the 1,000-metre-tall Puig de Galatzó. When cars snake through the narrow streets of the village in summer, many can barely stop, because the number of parking spaces is very limited. That is, of course, completely different in winter.

Mariano Navares, born in Miranda de Ebro in the Burgos province in 1959, who trained as a blacksmith and later studied interior design in Madrid, has lived as an artist on Mallorca from 1995 and settled in Estellencs over 20 years ago, fascinated by the Mediterranean light and the special location of the village. Navares works in an unusual studio in the middle of the village, opposite the town hall and next to the church, in an old, partially empty church building that was planned but never completed. He transformed it into his workshop and creates his art here with welding machines, files and hacksaws. Old engine blocks, crankshafts, shock absorbers, body parts and screws, combined with stainless steel and bronze elements, are composed into fantasy objects, but in many cases they are also figurative and representational.

Address Plaza Nueva, 07192 Estellencs, +34 (0)619 487066 (studio of the artist Mariano Navares) | **Getting there** On the Ma-10 from Valldemossa via Banyalbufar or coming from Andratx | **Hours** Donkey and sculpture in front of the studio always viewable, studio on request | **Tip** In front of the artist's studio stands his piece *Re Aczion A* from 2005, a 3.6-metre-tall, slim figure made of recycled materials and scrap metal, partially coloured, as well as *El Viajero Perdido* with suitcases from 1999.

34 __ Son Muda Gardens
The special sculpture park

This must be the most eccentric sculpture park on the island, initiated privately and developed with love. Dozens of renowned artists present their work on the large area of land here. A magnificent group of women by the acclaimed Joan Bennàssar is on view, alongside musical instruments by the Mallorquin sculptor Pedro Flores (dotted around an intriguing white garden), the masks of Pep Sirvent and the butterflies of Anatoly Neznamov. Almost all of them are made of stone, steel and bronze.

The splendid garden is continuously complemented with new works of art. It is open to the public once a year, on the first Saturday in May, under the motto 'Flores y Arte'. Then, interested visitors can visit the ingeniously laid out Son Muda garden, blossoming and green, enjoy the art, but also buy it. Otherwise the exciting garden can only be viewed by appointment.

It is, after all, a kind of showroom, or better still a show-garden for the landscaping company based in the finca, Son Muda Gardens, belonging to the Swiss couple Christian and Hélène Lindgens, who bought the finca as a ruin in 2010 and made a botanical feast for the eyes out of the 15,000-square-metre plot. Not only that: Hélène Lindgens realises her passion for garden landscaping and design here. In the meantime, Son Muda Gardens is one of the top addresses on the island for the planning, design, cultivation and upkeep of upmarket gardens, with 45 employees at present. Hélène Lindgens and her first landscape gardener Hans Achilles stand for the know-how to create high-class and ecologically sustainable gardens. A few dozen gardens are looked after, new creations are constantly added to the portfolio, also beyond the shores of Mallorca. Her aim: to create quality gardens that still suit the geological and meteorological conditions of the island and the periodic lack of water.

Address Diseminado Primera Volta 180, 07209 Felanitx, +34 (0)671 669001, www.sonmuda.com | **Getting there** Country road Ma-5110 Felanitx–Vilafranca, kilometre 8.4 | **Hours** Only upon request and by appointment, +34 (0)671 669001, sonmuda@gmail.com | **Tip** The seven windmills on the eastern hills of Felanitx, lined up like a pearl necklace, are worth seeing. Moli de N'Hereu is completely preserved. It is also worth taking a look at Sant Miquel church with its huge flight of stairs.

35___ The Statue of Christ

The Lord's greetings from Puig de Sant Salvador

If you intend to drive up the Puig de Sant Salvador in summer, you might end up in a bit of a sweat. The four-kilometre stretch of winding mountain road is narrow, difficult to read, and seems to go on for ever. Manoeuvring on this road requires skill and nerves in equal measure. Especially for those who can afford to experience this mountain in the off-season or even in winter. The drive up the 509-metre-tall mountain with its cross, which you can make out from far off on the deep plains, is a very special experience. Two larger-than-life size Christian symbols await you here, alongside a breath-taking view over large parts of Mallorca.

First you pass a huge stone cross dating back to 1957, which you can also climb up to when it's storming, and that is often the case up here. Even more imposing than the cross is the seven-metre-tall statue of Christ on the other side of the mountain, towering on top of a large plinth and an over 30-metre-tall column, constructed in 1937. The Santuari de Sant Salvador cloister, founded in 1342 and an important pilgrimage site for Mallorquins for hundreds of years, awaits, since the departure of the monks, with a small hotel and a good restaurant.

In a lobby of the cloister you will see six world champion jerseys belonging to the racing cyclist Guillermo Timoner, an idol of the 1950s and 1960s, who came from Felanitx. The Mallorquins venerate their world champion, whose former fame is comparable with that of their current sports idol, Rafael Nadal. But the focal point of the mountain is the monastery church, ornamented in baroque style in the 18th century, whose origins go back to the 14th century, when much of the population of Felanitx was killed by the plague and the survivors built a church in thanks for their salvation. When the stream of pilgrims got out of hand, the larger church was eventually built.

Address Puig de Sant Salvador, Monasterio de Sant Salvador, 07200 Felanitx | Getting there Exit from the road from Portocolom to Felanitx | Hours Mountain always accessible, contact the hotel on: +34 (0)971 515260 | Tip Towards Tramuntana it's worth visiting the town of Mancor de la Vall and Santa Llúcia monastery high above the town with its wonderful views. Ideal at sunset.

36__ The Tabletop Mountain

The nobility fled up here to escape the people

Mallorca has a tabletop mountain. It doesn't have the impact of the one in Cape Town, but it passes as a miniature version. You can make it out when you come from the south, and it stands rather perplexingly in the landscape. Even from down below, the ruins of Castells de Santueri appear in rough outline form. The journey up there is an experience in itself. The road is narrow and uneven and therefore little used, the landscape right and left of the road a feast for the eyes. What then awaits you up on the edge of the 400-metre-tall plateau is a piece of Roman, Arab and later Spanish history, in which you can completely immerse yourself – because time has stood still here. Over the centuries, almost nothing has been changed structurally on the stout defensive complex, largely castle ruins, which however are predominantly closed off for safety reasons. You can only go as far as the gate, but this does nothing to spoil the overwhelming impression.

The old lords of the castle will have seen the enemy coming from a long way off. Already in the Roman era, in around 100 BC, there was a defence tower on the mountain; after the conquest by the Arabs, a fortress was built. During the Reconquista, James I conquered the Castell after an intense siege and almost completely razed it. From the 14th century the fortress was built up again as a safe haven from the ever-increasing number of pirate raids. In the 1520s it finally served the landed gentry as a refuge during the bloody uprisings of the artisan guilds and the rural population against the oppressive taxing regime, the so-called Revolt of the Brotherhoods. From the 18th century, the fortress was left in the hands of nature. Now, the complete complex is to be lavishly restored and the tabletop mountain made accessible to the public. A worthwhile undertaking for a historic structure in the best of locations.

Address Castell de Santueri, 07200 Felanitx | Getting there From Felanitx on the Ma-4010 towards Portocolom or on the Ma-14 to Santanyí | Hours The gate is only opened sporadically. If it is closed, you can ask for the key at the Sa Possecio d'es Castell farm at the foot of the mountain. | Tip The old town around the harbour in Portocolom, the city that Christopher Columbus apparently came from, is worth seeing.

37 __ The Blue Youth Choir

A choir from Lluc monastery has achieved fame

The whole thing seems like an apparition. Around 40 boys in white-blue robes appear out of the blue in front of the black Madonna, spontaneously take up their positions and begin to sing like angels. Two chorales, less than 10 minutes long, and they disappear, the same way they came. A ritual that occurs several times a week at 11.15am on the dot in the basilica of Santuari de Lluc. An impression that continues to have an effect for a long time afterwards. Ave Maria de Lluc.

The choirboys are called 'Els Blauets', 'the blues'. And what very few people know is that this is one of the oldest choirs in Europe. In 1526, the prior of the monastery at the time decided that some boys should regularly sing in the early mass. The choir arose from this a few years later and the ritual of the daily performance, the 'Salve Regina' and a 'praise be' to Mallorca, that belongs to the strong spirituality surrounding the 'Moreneta', the black Madonna, which is venerated on the island like no other statue. The Lluc monastery is the centre of adoration of the Virgin Mary on Mallorca and the most important destination for pilgrims.

All of the choirboys, and for a few years now also a number of girls, are pupils of one of the most renowned schools on Mallorca, Escolania de Lluc, a monastery school with boarding, which has existed since 1532. The youngsters live here and, receive both an intensive musical and instrumental education and a complete academic education here.

Some 40 to 50 'Blauets' are active in the choir at any time. And due to their distinctive uniforms they are called 'the blues' to this day. The choir always performs in these flamboyant clothes, even when they set off during school holidays for performances outside the monastery, in numerous churches and cathedrals of large European cities, for example in Westminster Abbey in London.

Address Santuari de Lluc, Plaça dels Peregrins 1, 07315 Lluc, +34 971 871525 | Getting there From Inca on the Ma-2130 | Hours Daily 10am–6pm; the choir performs daily at 11.15am and during Sunday Mass | Tip The botanical gardens behind the monastery are particularly recommended.

38 Cap Blanc

Where the island shows off its wildest side

An unadulterated landscape awaits visitors to Cap Blanc. Bizarre, enormous, dizzying. Here the island tumbles precipitously into the sea. You drive the 16 kilometres from Llucmajor – the last part of the route on a dead-end street through an untouched nature reserve – and at some point you'll discover the white lighthouse Far de Blanc in front of you.

You can park your car here, jump over a small wall a little further on the right-hand side, and suddenly find yourself in the middle of the most fascinating island landscape. You can get close to the rugged cliff edge, but should be aware of the dangers. Here the landscape is rugged and stony, the scrub low, and there are reptiles. A springboard for breathtaking walks on the plateau, where there's a very special freshness to the wind. The sunsets here become unforgettable experiences.

The Far des Cap Blanc lighthouse, built 85 metres above sea level directly on the edge of the coast, came into operation in August 1863 and still provides a critical signal for shipping on the most southeasterly point of the Bay of Palma to this day. It was built by the engineer Emili Pou y Bonet (1830–1888), who was also responsible for the port facility in Palma and 20 other lighthouses on the Balearic Islands. The signal lighting of the tower was originally run on olive oil, then modernised time and again over the decades and ultimately electrified in 1970. Today, the LED lights blink every five seconds. The lighthouse was continuously inhabited until 1994.

In the broader area around the lighthouse you will come across numerous secret tunnels belonging to an old military battery, which are not officially open to the public. There is a bunker that can be accessed within walking distance of the tower. Setting off in an easterly direction, you can also hike to Cala Pi, past the towering 16th-century Cap Blanc defence tower.

Address 07639 Llucmajor (between El Arenal and Cala Pi) | Getting there From Llucmajor on the Ma-6015 towards S'Estanyol, in Venissa turn right onto the Ma-6014 and to the coast, or from El Arenal on the Ma-6014 | Hours Lighthouse always viewable from the outside | Tip There is a wonderful walk from the S'Estanyol yacht harbour to Far d'es Estallela and on to Cala Pi. It's worth visiting the bay of Cala Pi with its attractive beach surrounded by high walls and cliffs.

39 The Fig Finca

The passion of the pharmacist

This man is obsessed. In the most positive sense. Since pharmacist Montserrat Pons dedicated himself and his life completely to the fig 25 years ago, the fruit has determined his every thought and action. The man from Llucmajor, who still works as a pharmacist, bought the 130-hectare Son Mut Nou estate around nine kilometres southwest, a rather rugged, barely fertile area with mainly dry clay, with low-lying bushes and cacti. Perfect for the fig tree, which flourishes splendidly in barren and dry loam.

The sweetest and most aromatic fruit of its species grow particularly well here. Some 80 years ago, Mallorca was the number one producer of figs worldwide.

Driven by science, Montserrat Pons set up a project here that is definitely one of a kind. In the meantime, the 65-year-old pharmacist has planted more than 3,000 fig trees in over 1,000 varieties from 60 countries around the world – including the Americas, Greece, Egypt, Australia and Japan – on 130 hectares of land. An unbelievable 260 of them are solely from the Balearic Islands. Son Mut Nou is a huge experimental laboratory focused on the fig. Pons researches the form, colour and taste of the fruit in greenhouses built especially for the purpose next to the fig plantations near the finca. Everything is keenly tagged, catalogued and photographed.

Harvest time for figs is in the months August and September. Visitors are cordially welcome. For a contribution of €5 the host and his staff offer guided tours and introduce visitors to the history and science of fig growing. Included in the price: a kilo of figs of your choice from the extensive range. Furthermore, fig lovers can buy many different fig products: fig jam, fig bread, fig vinegar, fig beer and fig tea obtained from fig tree leaves, all of it homemade. And on the large patio you can enjoy all kinds of delicacies related to and featuring the fig.

Address Son Mut Nou, Camí des Palmer, 07609 Llucmajor, +34 (0)646 633259 | Getting there From Palma on the Ma-19, take exit 22 (Llucmajor–Algaida) on the Ma-6020, first road after the roundabout on the right into Camí de Se Torre, after around 3 kilometres turn right onto Camí des Palmer, through the gate onto the car park by the house | Hours Tue, Thu & Sat 8am–1pm, booking for guided tours recommended | Tip On Carretera Cabo Blanco, kilometre 40, near Campos is the Artestruz ostrich farm with lots of South African flair.

40 Sant Bonaventura
Monastic symbiosis

It is not quite what one would expect in Llucmajor, the former stronghold of the shoemaking trade, situated far away from the coast: a highly modern cultural and education centre in the middle of a medieval monastery complex. Away from the town centre between small alleyways, in a rather inconspicuous area. A project like no other on the island, and yet a hot tip not only for native culture vultures. Watching concerts here in the cloister on summer evenings or visiting one of the top-class exhibitions, allows you to enjoy island life from the other side.

Sant Bonaventura monastery was founded by the Franciscans in 1608 and was expanded time and again in the following decades. The church and cloister was added to by several annexes and a vegetable garden. The Franciscans taught religion and theology here and developed the monastery into a centre for Christian faith outside of Palma. Life played out around the two-storey cloister with its dozens of monastic cells and communal rooms. This came to an abrupt end with secularisation and nationalisation in 1836. For over 150 years, until 1998, the monastery was used as a recovery room of the Guardia Civil, as a hospice, prison and also as a communal abattoir. The complex was repeatedly tinkered with and built on. The old monastery deteriorated and became ruinous in several places. At the beginning of the 2000s the monastery was finally rededicated, declared a national cultural asset, extensively restored and began fulfilling its new purpose in 2007.

Most importantly the precious murals, which had been whitewashed over, were discovered in 1999 by a group of historians. They have now been exposed as iconographic testimony of the history of the Franciscan order. The white, grey and black holy images uncovered in the colonnade, created using the Grisaille painting technique, are thought to be unique on Mallorca.

Address Claustre de Sant Bonaventura, Carrer Fra Joan Garau 1, 07620 Llucmajor,
+34 (0)971 669758 | Getting there From Palma on the Ma-19 or the Ma-19A to Llucmajor |
Hours Mon–Fri 9am–2pm & 4–8pm, Sat 9am–2pm, entrance free | Tip On the small
square opposite the church is the bronze statue *S'Espigolera* ('The young corn gleaner') from
1965, by the sculptor Horacio de Eguia, who wanted to honour the work of the Mallorquin
poet Maria Antònia Salvà.

41 The Olive Plantation

The island's gold grows in Aubocassa

The history of the Aubocassa estate stretches right back to the 12th century, and when you arrive there, a few kilometres beyond Manacor on the small country road, you may think you've walked straight onto a film set.

An old, manor-like estate with its own small church, framed by cypress trees and surrounded by broad olive groves. This estate now belongs to Bodegas Roda, a company at home in Haro (La Rioja) on the Spanish mainland, who have constructed their own branch for oil production here. The wine makers are doing what has distinguished Mallorca for centuries in grand style in Aubocassa: growing olives. The plantation is made up of around 8,000 olive trees of the Arbequína variety on an area of 24 hectares. Eight kilograms of olives are processed to make a litre of oil; 60,000 bottles of oil are produced annually, of which around 80 per cent are consumed in Spain.

Olive trees are as much part of the island's image as the wind and water mills, but in this case they have been around for ages. In fact, the Phoenicians are thought to have brought the first olive trees to Mallorca a good 3,000 years ago. And since then these bizarre crooked figures have borne silent witness to entire epochs of history. Many of these olive trees are up to 500 or even 1,000 years old. Those cultivated for oil production are of course younger and more productive. They grow well in the Mediterranean climate, and are robust against the wind, weather and natural pests. The oil comes in various flavours and is also of differing quality. Since the 16th century, olive trees have been systematically used for agriculture. The olives are harvested as fresh as possible, best of all in November. They are processed just a few hours after picking, using cold centrifuging, so without subsequent filtering. In Aubocassa you really can get a feel for the oil production process.

Address Camí de Son Fangós, kilometre 7, 07500 Manacor, +34 (0)971 100388, www.aubocassa.com | Getting there Coming from Palma on the Ma-15 to Manacor, then at the end of town turn into Camì de Son Fangós to kilometre 7 | Hours Mon–Fri 9am–1pm & 3–5pm. Viewing tours with tasting by appointment at www.aubocassa.com. | Tip The Solivellas family produces one of Mallorca's best olive oils on their estate Es Guinyent near Alcúdia (+34 (0)971 545722, www.olisolivettas.com). There are also a lot of olives grown around Sóller.

42 — The Rafa Nadal Museum
The hero of the island's tennis camp

What Rafael Nadal, who was born into an enthusiastic sports family in 1986 and is currently the most famous son of the island, has created at the gates of his birth place Manacor is definitely worth taking a look at. The Rafa Nadal Sports Centre extends over an area of over 40,000 square metres and offers an ultramodern sports and tennis complex through the Rafa Nadal Academy. Over 40 instructors and trainers work on 26 tennis courts and numerous other sports pitches. In addition, there is the organisation of congresses and meetings. The weekly training programmes, exclusively for adults, are conducted at all levels, from beginner to top athlete. Then there are the regular tennis tournaments for participants. The course participants live in an in-house hotel, that has an indoor and an outdoor pool as well as a large spa area.

With the Rafa Nadal Museum Xperience, the 19-times Grand Slam winner has provided the island with a high-tech museum with sales shop. You make your way inside through a video-animated corridor, with showy sounds. On an interactive floor with numerous simulators, the visitors can actively immerse themselves in the world of a professional sportsperson and compete with one another, whether in tennis or rowing, in Formula 1 or in cycling. On the lower floor of the museum, almost everything is about Rafael Nadal, who welcomes the visitor in an animation in three languages. Cups, medals and tennis accessories from his career are on show as well as an historic collection of tennis rackets from other masters of the sport. For example, Boris Becker's first racket. But also the original racing car of the Spanish Formula 1 world champion Fernando Alonso from 2005, Sebastian Vettel's original helmet and Usain Bolt's running shoes.

You can enjoy a great view of the outdoor facilities from the restaurant's large terrace.

Address Rafa Nadal Sports Centre, Carretera Calas de Mallorca, 07500 Manacor, 971/171680, www.rafanadalacademy.com | **Getting there** From Palma on the Ma-15 to Manacor; bus 411 or 412 to the Museum | **Hours** Rafa Nadal Museum Xperience: Apr–Oct daily 10am–6.30pm, Nov–Mar daily 10am–2.30pm, admission every 30 minutes, maximum 25 people | **Tip** Manacor is famous for the manufacture of artificial pearls, including Perlas Majorica. If you drive from Manacor towards the sea, you will come across the Coves dels Hams and the 'dragon cave' Coves del Drac with its subterranean Martel Lake.

43__Trotting Race Course
'Trot' in Manacor and Palma

Harness racing is extremely popular on Mallorca. On race days the Mallorquins come together at the trotting course in Palma or Manacor. A visit to one of the two race courses is worthwhile, because this is where you will experience Mallorca in its purest form. You don't need to be into horses or gambling. Harness racing, always at a trot, is lived on Mallorca, and there are many more horse owners than you might think, sprucing up their horses for the race course at home on the finca and then testing themselves against the competition on the track at the weekend. and possibly taking a few hundred euros home with them.

Trotting racing, always called 'trot' on Mallorca, has around 30,000 followers and is considered the number two sport on the island after football. Trot is a purely Balearic sport and completely unknown on the Spanish mainland, originating from farmer chariot races at the end of big market days. There are over 6,000 extremely passionate breeders of the Trotons, the trotting horses especially bred on the Balearics, and numerous stables are to be found especially in the east of the island, around Manacor. Horses train on small tracks around the fincas and during the week on the race courses in Manacor and Palma.

The trotting race course in Manacor was built in 1929 and has been modernised several times – now it is of course equipped with computers and electronic betting machines. At its heart, alongside the unreserved seating, is a large grandstand, partially behind glass, on three storeys. Betting is of course a highly motivating element, but the social value of these weekend events should not be underestimated. The most important, financially rewarding and prestigious race of the year is the Gran Premio Nacional on the trotting race course in Palma, on the third weekend in May. Only three-year-old horses born in Spain are allowed to compete.

Address Hipòdrom de Manacor, 07500 Manacor, +34 (0)971 823492 | Getting there On the Palma–Artà road, kilometre 48 | Hours Races take place on Saturday or Sunday. Racing usually begins at 4pm | Tip Another trotting race course is the Hipòdrom Son Pardo in Palma. Find out about race dates on Mallorca at the Federación Balear de Trote, Carretera de Sóller, kilometre 3.5 (Hipòdrom Son Pardo, 07009 Palma, +34 (0)971 468508, office hours Mon–Fri 8am–3pm, www.federaciobaleardetrot.com).

44 Plaça de Toros

Bullfighting still takes place here

The city of Muro, which has a little over 7,000 inhabitants, wishes to hold on to the Corrida, the organisation of bullfights, unperturbed by all the protest that the bloody spectacle now evokes across the island. Bullfighting not only raises the hackles of most tourists, but also evermore Mallorquins, primarily of course local animal rights activists and especially young people. The debate for and against the Corrida was ignited in 2011 by the legally enacted ban on bullfighting in Catalonia, whose expansion to the Balearic Islands was vehemently demanded. But the autonomous region of Mallorca does not want to be told what to do and for the time being has retained this Spanish tradition.

Whether bullfighting takes place or not, their arena is certainly holy to the 'Mureros', the citizens of Muro. And they still eagerly await the annual Corrida on 24 June, the day of the patron saint San Joan Baptiste. Tickets for the 6,000-seater 'La Monumental' and the traditional six fights with three Toreros are always sold out in no time. This day has been one of the highlights in the otherwise rather uneventful city, since the influential citizen Jaime Serra Palau decided to build a bullfighting arena here at the start of the 1920s. And it was a big hit. The arena was to be created in a large quarry. No sooner said than done. Except it took several years until the circular arena with a diameter of 37.5 metres was chiselled out deep below ground level and the circular seating painstakingly pounded into the rock. There's no other arena in the whole of Spain to compare with La Monumental in Muro.

And for Spanish bullfighters, 'Monumental de Muro' is a venue at which you must fight at least once in your career. The Muro arena was taken over from private ownership by the municipality for €500,000 in 2010. Extensively renovated, it presents itself today in renewed splendour.

Address La Monumental, Plaça de Toros, 07440 Muro, +34 (0)971 860826 | Getting there From Manacor via Santa Margalida, from Palma via Inca and Sa Pobla | Hours Enquire about events, but the arena can also be viewed from the outside | Tip Alongside La Monumental in Muro from 1918 there is Coliseo Balear in Palma (1929), Plaça de Toros de Alcúdia (1892), La Macarena in Felanitx (1914) and Plaça de Toros in Inca (1910), since 2008 with the bullfighting museum Museo Taurino.

45 — The Estate

Comassema offers unique insights

On a map of Mallorca created in 1785 on behalf of the then cardinal Antoni Despuig, it becomes startlingly evident just how rich the island was in large and small estates in the preindustrial era. There are some 1,250 stately properties registered on it, from fincas to large agricultural enterprises, of which around 300 function as agro-hotels, guesthouses or vineyards today. The Possessións, the large estates, were the main employees for most Mallorquins and their families for centuries. The landowners were some of the most influential people on the island. One of these feudal estates is Possessió Comassema in the Orient valley in the Tramuntana mountain range. When you visit the estate, which has been self-sufficient over the centuries, prepare yourself for a sensory trip back in time that will help you begin to understand the original structures of the island. Comassema, first mentioned in 1229 during the period of the island's recapture from the Moors by James I, belonged for a long time to the Palou de Comassema family, until it came into the possession of the family of the current host, Fernando Fortuny Salas, in 1891.

It was he who was able to persuade his family to use the private property – alongside agriculture, in which the olive harvest still plays a dominant role – for the purpose of tourism, and in parts make it accessible to the public, also for events, such as parties and weddings. He joined the initiative 'Itinerem', whose aim is to promote and preserve cultural activities around the island's historic estates.

A visit to Comassema is a delight. You see the cultivated gardens with the fruit, citrus and olive trees, some of which are thousands of years old, the historical rooms, the old oil mill – once powered by donkeys, then electrified – which is still in operation, the huge 4,600-cubic-metre water basins and the palm groves.

Address Finca Comassema, Camino Privado, 07349 Orient, +34 (0)971 180117 | Getting there On the small road from Alaró to Orient, around 100 metres after the end of the town turn right at the fork to Finca Comassema, around 3 kilometres along the path; booking requested, otherwise gate to the estate will be closed | Hours Only by appointment, +34 (0)971 180117, www.fincascomassema.com, organised guided tours: Ingrid Flohr, +34 (0)690 218709, www.galeriaflohr@gmx.net | Tip Visit Fundacíon Itinerem (contact: Diego Zaforteza Torruella, +34 (0)672 394431, www.fundacion-itinerem.org). The estates Sollerich near Alaró, Sa Coma near Valldemossa and Can Bosch near Pollenca are also in the Itinerem programme. The nearby picturesque mountain village of Orient is one of the prettiest villages on the island.

46   The Arms Museum

Calm amid the arms

Twice a year, the ocean liner *Queen Mary 2* is welcomed to the port of Palma. When that happens, the world's largest cruiseship seems to fill the Porto Pi terminal to bursting point.

In season, however, regular cruiseships form part of the daily life of this part of Palma. Above the mooring places of cruisers and ocean liners, the time-honoured Castell de Sant Carles (1610) on the peninsula, once the fortification of Porto Pui, holds the island's arms and military museum.

For those interested in Spanish history, and Mallorcan history in particular, this museum, opened in 1981, is a treat – despite the many weapons and a history full of armed conflict. There are fabulous views across the Bay of Palma from the roof of the completely restored Castell, amidst numerous historic howitzers and cannons giving you an idea of how enemy ships were greeted from this defensive position. Until 1980, the castle was used as an artillery barracks and military prison.

Today, the visitor is greeted by numerous rooms inside the fortification, the visit starting from the courtyard below the tall watchtower. The collection of war artefacts and military equipment spans the Middle Ages to the 20th century (including, impressively, a World War II Enigma machine), but holds some older pieces too from the time of the Knights Templar and the Reconquista. The miniature battlefield with hundreds of figures representing Hannibal's army is impressive.

Even if military memorabilia is not your thing you'll enjoy the visit, as despite all the armaments, the castle exudes an immense calm and everything is far less menacing than you might think.

There is always a fresh breeze blowing up here at this elevation, and the café under pine trees is a cosy place for a rest. The museum often hosts enjoyable classical concerts in the courtyard.

Address Muscu Històric Militar de les Balears, Castell de Sant Carles, Carrer Dock West, Dic de l'Oest, 07015 Palma de Mallorca, Porto Pi, +34 (0)971 402145 | Getting there Bus 1 to Dic de l'Oest (last stop) | Hours Mon–Fri 9am–1pm, Sat 10am–1pm | Tip Make sure you take a stroll along the harbour walk with its fishing port, the royal yacht club and the marina. Boat trips around the harbour or for the day are also on offer here.

47 — Babel Bookshop
Browsing in a stylish atmosphere

This bookshop is a gem. It mainly stocks books in Spanish and Catalan, but also has a selection in English and German. And there is an extensive collection of coffee-table books, a music library and numerous bibliophile rarities. In total, the range includes around 20,000 titles specialising in the humanities, with books ranging from mythology and poetry to travel writing. On top of that there is also a series of literature and art journals. You will definitely get your money's worth here – even if you don't buy anything. It's the unusual location that makes this bookshop so attractive, along with the upbeat atmosphere, accentuated by jazz music, and the relaxation you find here, only a few steps away from the hectic Carrer Sant Miquel.

The bookseller and former philosophy teacher José Luis Martínez opened the Babel bookshop in a renovated townhouse on the small but exclusive Plaça Arabí 10 years ago. The inspiration for the choice of name was Jorge Luis Borges' story *La Biblioteca de Babel* (*The Library of Babel*). Inside, the bookshop mirrors the rooms of an old townhouse; the rooms are not very tall, the ceilings bulge under massive wooden beams and the areas join together, divided by small steps, with parquet flooring throughout. A piano stands ready to be played at any time.

Babel is also a café. You can drink coffee or eat tapas at the bar or at one of the bistro tables dotted throughout the bookshop, but the menu also contains a large variety of drinks. And you can browse at the same time. The bookshop is also a wine bar. In a large temperature-controlled wine cabinet there are 200 wines to choose from. Alongside selected Mallorquin wines, there are also wines from the owner's home region, Ribera del Duero in northern Spain. But the highlight of the bookshop has to be the slightly rounded wooden sun terrace outside, made for savouring and browsing.

Address La Biblioteca de Babel, Carrer de Arabí, 07003 Palma de Mallorca, +34 (0)971 721442, www.labibliotecadebabel.es | Getting there From Plaça Major in towards Plaça d'Espanya at Basilica de Sant Miquel | Hours Wed–Sat 10am–10pm | Tip Another good bookshop (and one with a small stock of English books) is Literanta at Carrer Can Fortuny 4 near Santa Eulalia with a bar and a cosy reading corner. They also run creative writing workshops.

48 The Barceló Chapel
Modern art in Palma's old cathedral

The Spanish royal couple were there and with them a large delegation of Catalan dignitaries and artists. In February 2007, the 700-year-old Palma cathedral, one of the most magnificent sacred buildings of Gothic architecture in Spain and Europe, located high above the old town, experienced the inauguration of a quite extraordinary work of art: the over-sized ceramic work by the Mallorquin artist Miquel Barceló. Palma has since been an attraction richer, even though access to this contemporary work is closed off to many visitors.

Miquel Barceló from Felanitx, born in 1957, received the contract to design the Saint Peter chapel (Capella de Sant Pere) at the end of the cathedral's right side aisle with a motif from the New Testament in 2000 from the former bishop of Palma, Teodoro Úbeda. The contract for a contemporary abstract work of art in the venerable cathedral was all the more astounding as Barceló is considered a critic of religion.

The result was a 300-square-metre mural of clay and ceramics that covers almost the whole chapel. The Biblical story of the miraculous 'multiplication of bread and fish' during the feeding of the five thousand is symbolised within it.

The imposing, 16-metre-tall wall relief shows a suggested Jesus figure, flanked by everything that the sea has to offer: waves and surf with fish gasping for air, which suddenly appear on the surface of the sea, as well as loaves of bread and shoals of fish. The five glass windows, designed by Barceló in dark blue and grey, symbolise the interior of the sea. He has achieved a work of art here that feels very much like it emerged from this island. It is most definitely controversial, like the work of his famous predecessor Antoni Gaudí, who redesigned the cathedral at the beginning of the 20th century and whose artistic accents it is hard to imagine the world without.

Address Catedral de la Seu, Plaça Almoina, 07001 Palma de Mallorca | Getting there
On foot, take the steps up from Passeig des Born | Hours Apr–May, Oct Mon–Fri
10am–5.15pm, June–Sept Mon–Fri 10am–6.15pm, Nov–Mar 10am–3.15pm; all year
Sat 10am–2.15pm | Tip The walls of the royal chapel with its glass ceramics are by Antoni
Gaudí, as are the heptagonal baldachin above the high altar, the music cherubs and the
choir stalls. The Portal del Mirador, the 14th-century Gothic entrance, is worth a look.

49__Calatrava's Bull
Avant-garde art on the city wall

The Bou, the bull, high up on the city wall at Es Baluard museum is visible from afar and is increasingly becoming an emblem of the city. The Spanish king Juan Carlos and his wife came to town especially for the inauguration of this unusual sculpture by the architect Santiago Calatrava. The occasion for the ceremonial unveiling of this gigantic bronze sculpture, made up of 50 individual pieces, on the roof of the Es Baluard, was the three-year anniversary of the museum, an important exhibition space for modern and contemporary art.

The extravagant Calatrava sculpture, which has a total weight of 30 tonnes and a height of 15 metres, was delivered by several heavy-load vehicles and heaved and mounted onto the wall with special cranes. It is made up of five staggered, almost two-metre-tall and wide stacked cubes, climbing up towards the heavens, standing on two abstract bull's horns and held by a bold steel construction.

The highly successful architect, building engineer and sculptor Santiago Calatrava is one of the stars of the contemporary art and culture scene. One of his specialities: the construction of spectacular bridge structures, of railway stations and airport terminals, congress centres and theatres such as the opera house in Valencia as well as skyscrapers such as the twisting Turning Torso in Malmö, Sweden. All of Calatrava's constructions and sculptures have one thing in common: they always move the viewer emotionally. No one seems to manage to stroll past a Calatrava untouched.

The master of modern architecture, born in 1951 near Valencia, always works with the most up-to-date technology and is constantly experimenting with new artistic forms. The most important inspiration at the start of his career was his intellectual dialogue with the work of the legendary architect Le Corbusier. Many experts consider him the logical successor to Antoni Gaudí.

Address Plaça de la Porta de Santa Catalina 10, 07012 Palma de Mallorca,
+34 (0)971 908200, www.esbaluard.org | **Getting there** On foot two minutes from Passeig
Mallorca; bus 1–7, 20 or 50, to Es Baluard and by tourist bus | **Hours** The museum's
observation deck, on which the sculpture is to be found, is freely accessible. Museum:
Tue–Sat 10am–8pm, Sun 10am–3pm | **Tip** Es Baluard museum for modern and
contemporary art is a must. It shows work by artists such as Pablo Picasso and Joan Miró,
Rebecca Horn and Gerhard Richter. There is also an unusual sculpture park. Spending the
sunset having a drink on the terrace of the Es Baluard is pure pleasure.

50___ Call Major
Once a centre of Jewish life

Call Major was the largest medieval Jewish quarter in Palma. Long ignored, this area of the city in the shadow of the cathedral is being increasingly rediscovered, as is Call Menor behind Santa Eulalia church. Both quarters are only signposted nowadays – the old courses the roads used to take can only be guessed at: in Call Major around the Monte Sión church, which stands where the largest synagogue in the city was once located, and in Call Menor along Carrer de l'Argenteria. All of this is hard to find and requires patience and intuition.

Help can be found in the form of the small information centre for Jewish culture and history in Carrer Almudaina, Centre Maimó ben Faraig, which opened in 2015. It is named after Maimó ben Faraig, an influential Jew who lived in this building in the 13th century when the island was under Muslim rule, before being banished by the Christians. It also houses a tiny museum, which exhibits old texts on Jewish life in Palma, a seven-armed candelabra as tall as a man and the remains of the old Roman city wall, thanks to a series of maps and photographs.

Pogroms, death, persecution and the expulsion of Mallorca's Jews accompanied the victory of the Christians over Muslim rule. The uncompromising decree that included the expulsion or the conversion of Jews to the Catholic faith was issued in around 1430. Thousands of Jews on Mallorca were forced to become Catholic, just in order to survive. But the Xuetas, as they were pejoratively called, were never accepted by the Mallorquin Catholics. They remained for the rest of their lives and for generations to come right up into the 20th century the 'Jews' who lived out their faith in secret. They were ostracised and marginalised. But in fact, despite forced conversion, many Xuetas have preserved their Jewish identity. To this day around 20,000 Mallorquins bear Xueta names.

Address Centre Maimó ben Faraig, Carrer de l'Almudaina 9, 07001 Palma de Mallorca, +34 (0)971 225599 | **Getting there** In front of the cathedral through Carrer del Palau Reial into Carrer de l'Almudaina | **Hours** Mon–Fri 9.30am–1.30pm, organised sightseeing walks Sat 10am and noon, +34 (0)971 225599 | **Tip** At the end of 2018 the German artist Gunter Demning began laying 'stumbling blocks' in Palma, in memory of the Mallorquins abducted through national socialism and the Franco dictatorship and murdered predominantly in German concentration camps. There are seven memorial stones on Plaça de la Pescateria on Carrer de Colom.

51__ Can Balanguer
A taste of the aristocratic life

Patio tours through the old town of Palma are very informative if you want to get an insight into the lives of old, aristocratic, well-to-do Mallorquin families. The city is rich in chic city houses, patrician and aristocratic palaces with lush planted courtyards, which are often converted into classy hotels, shopping temples and galleries after thorough and purpose-driven renovation. One gets a sense of how the well-heeled nobles may once have lived.

However, you won't find a more vividly enlightening glance into the life of the Mallorquin upper class than a visit to the historic old town palace Can Balanguer, a stone's throw away from Plaça a Rei Joan Carlos I. After an elaborate renovation over many years, strictly preserving the old character, the palace became accessible once again in 2019. At the centre of this magnificent Baroque building from the first half of the 18th century, containing one of the biggest courtyards in the city, used for diverse cultural events, is the permanent exhibition 'La casa possible'. The visitor strolls through the swanky, spacious rooms of the Balanguer family. The musician, businessman and patron of the arts Joseph Balanguer (1869–1951) acquired the city palace, which had been converted time and again by its previous owners, in 1927 and furnished it according to his own design using the interior of the previous owner families. After his death, the Balanguer family gifted the building, subject to conditions, to the city of Palma.

Alongside the large hall, the fireside lounge and dining room and the spacious salon, the Balanguer's art collection along the corridors of the *piano nobile* stands out in particular, and includes some important works by contemporary Art Nouveau artists. But don't miss the music room with its old, artfully ornamented 'Walcker' chamber organ, which still rings out today when concerts are performed here.

Address Carrer de la Unió 3, 07001 Palma de Mallorca, +34 (0)971 225900 | Getting there Only a few metres away from Plaça a Rei Joan Carlos I at the end of Passeig des Born | Hours Tue–Sat 10am–7pm, Sun 11am–2pm | Tip You should definitely take a closer look at the old Grand Hotel, which boasts an imposing Art Nouveau façade, today's Fundación La Caixa. The same goes for the two Modernist houses of Edifici Casasayas, built between 1908 and 1911, with their curved façades.

52 The Candle Shop

All things holy in a small space

There are many Catholic processions in Palma, plenty of church feast days and religious rituals of all kinds. And they almost always involve candles from the over 120-year-old, tiny candlemaker Cerería La Real from the district of Es Secar de la Real. Here, Guillem Ramis and his son, the fourth generation of his family to do so, produce candles of all types and sizes, from baptism and communion candles to the enormous specimens for church altars. Easter is boom time and Passion Week is 'candle week'. Admittedly, you'll find evermore industrial candles and electric lights in the houses of God. After all, they are easier to care for and less expensive. The candles from the Cerería La Real factory are certainly not cheap, but they are of course of exquisite quality. They come in a wide variety of diameters and lengths, including many custom-made products with inscriptions for feast days. They also drip much less than industrial candles, burn more evenly and give off a wonderful light.

The small, eccentric sales shop on Plaça de l'Hospital, right next door to Hospital General, the modernised hospital from the Middle Ages, is worth seeing. Eighty per cent of the candles produced are sold here, frequently also to foreign guests. One candle can cost up to €80, depending on the size. They also have candles for parties and weddings on offer. The remaining candles go directly to the churches. Their main customers are the nearby Església de la Sang and La Seu cathedral, where Cerería La Real is responsible for the altar candles. A real accolade for a candlemaker.

But there is a lot more apart from candles in the shop. The place is bursting with hundreds of devotional objects such as rosary beads, angels and crosses, saints in snow globes, religious images in cans, Madonna and Jesus figures with and without halo, little cards with prayers and lucky charms.

Address Plaça de l'Hospital 2, 07012 Palma de Mallorca, +34 (0)696 278027 | Getting there Bus 4, 7, 20 or 35 to La Rambla / Via Roma | Hours Daily 8am–1pm & 4–8pm | Tip Art exhibitions take place regularly in the nearby Capella de la Misericòrdia, free admission.

53__ The Chocolatería

Where Joan Miró also slurped his chocolate

This café is considered the best Chocolatería in Palma and is the oldest and most traditional of its kind in the city. The same high-quality chocolate has been served here, in Art Nouveau decor and a touch of Biedermeier, under glass chandeliers of coloured glass, beside curved birdcages, slender vases, copper kettles and wooden cabinets, since the start of the 18th century. It all started, as the blue-and-white tiles in the café illustrate, in the year 1700, when Joan de S'Aigo had the idea of bringing ice down from the Tramuntana mountains from the snow houses or Cases de Neu to sell it, enriched with chocolate, in the city as ice cream in the most incredible creations.

Chocolatería Ca'n Joan de S'Aigo, hidden in Palma's narrow old town alleyways near the Santa Eulalia church, is a highlight for anyone with a bit of a sweet tooth. The 'black gold' in this chocolate oasis is mostly served thick and gooey, still steaming in cups and glasses and every imaginable variation. Then there are the small cakes (try the cremadillos or the delicious quartos), or homemade almond ice cream, made from locally milled almonds. Or better still: dunk a freshly baked Mallorquin ensaimada pastry into a cup of chocolate so thick a spoon could stand up in it! There is, of course, also a selection of coffees and, for refreshment so to speak, also cold drinks. And all of this at extremely affordable prices. No surprise that the Chocolatería fills up towards evening, especially with locals, among whom the café is extremely popular.

This place, with its green tiled palm branch floor and the plain tables with white marble slabs, where everything inclines towards the kitsch, has always attracted many artists, who were inspired by the unusual ambience and the unique atmosphere. Among the more well-known customers was the painter and sculptor Joan Miro, who would come in to drink his chocolate from time to time.

Address Carrer Can Sanç 10, 07001 Palma de Mallorca, +34 (0)971 710759 | Getting there Between Plaça Major and Santa Eulalia church | Hours Daily except Tue 8am – 9pm | Tip Ca'n Joan de S'Aigo now has two more branches in Palma: on Carrer del Baró de Santa Maria del Sepulcre and Carrer del Sidicat. Diagonally opposite, at Carrer Can Sanç 5, is the avant-garde theatre Teatre Sans.

54__The Delicatessen

The sausages of Colomado Santo Domingo

The 'land of milk and honey' is a fictional place in story and legend, in which everything to eat and drink is in plentiful supply. Once you have eaten your fill in this supposed paradise, make sure you don't end up like the figures in Pieter Bruegel's painting from 1567, who are depicted lying stupified on the floor, sleeping off the effects of their overindulgence.

There is a little bit of the land of milk and honey about Colomado Santo Domingo in Palma's old town, a small shop that has been here since 1886 and extends deep into the house like a tube. The shop, run by Pedro Amenguals, in the fourth generation of the family, cannot accommodate more than three customers at the same time, as it is stuffed full of delicacies.

There are 17 different sausage creations, original Mallorquin Sobrasadas, hanging from the ceiling, touching the customers if they don't duck down – as if the sausages want to fly straight into your mouth. The walls of the shop are also covered with Sobrasadas in all shapes and sizes: long, round, coiled. In between hang the Serrano hams. There are baskets full to bursting with grapes, oranges, strawberries, almonds and figs. Innumerable types of cheese line up, one after the other. You can find dried fruit, homemade jams, olive sticks and the delicious fig bread, numerous wines and sweet liquors. And everything is 'made in Mallorca', by the local agricultural finca.

The speciality of the shop, the core business, is of course the homemade 'Sobrasada de Mallorca porc negre', the sausage from black Mallorquin pork (with paprika), the native breed of pig. This speciality is only available on the island. The Colomado Santo Domingo is a visual highlight. But beware: please don't just take photographs, take some advice and try something. Perhaps also seize the opportunity and buy something. You won't satisfy your hunger by looking alone.

Address Carrer de Sant Domingo 1, 07001 Palma de Mallorca, +34 (0)971 714887,
www.colomadosantodomingo.com | Getting there Around 300 metres away from the
cathedral or Plaza de Cort | Hours Mon–Sat 10.30am–7.30pm | Tip The daily flower
market on the Rambla is worth a visit. A look at Plaça de Francesc de Garcia i Orell
with the bougainvillea-smothered roundabout and inviting benches is a pleasure.

55__The Franco Monument
The perennial row over a dark chapter of history

The municipal administration of Palma are reminded time and again that there are still a good two dozen street names and squares that bear the names of politicians and soldiers of the Franco dictatorship on signs and commemorative plaques. This should now finally be over. The city laid down the clearest statement in 2010 with the 20-metre-tall Francoist monument dominating Plaça de la Feixina, which was inaugurated in 1948 by General Franco himself. The largest and most controversial memorial of this kind on the Balearic Islands was not demolished, as numerous victims' associations and democratic initiatives demanded, but rededicated as a memorial against war. A compromise, with which those who see in these monoliths a piece of Mallorquin cultural history they want to preserve at all costs have ultimately asserted themselves. All Francoist symbols on memorials have been dismantled and ground down. Around the water basin that surround the monument, a rusty metal band was installed, into which lettering is embossed in various languages including English:

'This monument was erected in 1948, in memory of the victims of the sinking of the cruiser *Baleares* during the Spanish Civil War 1936–1939. Today it exemplifies the democratic will of the city, to never allow the horrors of war and dictatorships to be forgotten. Palma 2010.'

For many Mallorquins, this kind of reappraisal of Franco's fascism does not go far enough. Mallorca, which was captured by the Franco rebels straight after the rebellion against the central republican government in the summer of 1936, was also ambivalent towards Franco's reign of terror. The Mallorquin middle classes and the Catholic Church were the ones who always stood on the side of the Francoists and silenced any opposition. The Francoist Monument was also erected after World War II on their initiative.

Address Plaça de la Feixina, 07012 Palma de Mallorca | Getting there Bus 1 or 21 to Passeig de Mallorca or Carrer Argentina; on foot from Plaça Porta de Santa Catalina via Passeig de Mallorca beyond the city canal | Tip Plaça de la Feixina is a spacious park with numerous works of art, roaring cascades, palm trees and jacaranda trees, popular among skaters.

56 The Gargoyle on the Roof
Lookout over all the citizens

If you stroll along the narrow and dark Almudaina to Carrer Morei, it may be that you suddenly hear far-off laughter. Then you feel that you are being watched – associations race, medieval fantasies abound. It's no real surprise in this film-like setting. There it is again, that derisive smirk that sounds so mocking. There is no doubt that it comes from above. And if you look up between the tall houses and the gables, you can just about make it out: the grimacing wooden face, the mask, the teeth, the hair, the beard, the pointed ears. At least 30 metres up, under the overhanging wooden gable of this huge townhouse. Or is it all just your imagination? Perhaps the zoom lens of your camera will clear things up.

Apparently such figures, predominantly animal masks, were often mounted on the gables or façades of houses, in order to banish evil spirits, but sometimes also to garner favour from the spirits. People used to commission renowned sculptors, in the firm belief that life under such a roof would be safe and carefree. And then there are the carvings that burst with irony.

One of the most striking examples is to be found at Carrer Sant Feliu 10 in the lower old town. Here you pass by the medieval house Can Pavesi, later in Italian ownership, furnished with a new façade. Masks, grimaces and a face, half human, half lion, hang over the door. And this artfully sculptured head is sticking its tongue out at you. This should clearly signal to those who look up and talk rubbish or make fun of what they see: 'For he who passes'. At least that is what is written beneath it.

Since then the house in Palma has also been called Les Carasses, which means 'The Masks'. This kind of façade or building ornamentation came to Palma from Italy in the 18th century and was initially employed by Italian house owners as an artistic stylistic device, that was ultimately adapted by the Mallorquins.

Address Corner of Carrer Almudaina/Carrer Morei, 07001 Palma de Mallorca | Getting there From Plaça de Cort over Plaça Santa Eulàlia into Morei and on the left side there | Tip In the Renaissance palace Palau Aiamans (Carrer de la Portella 5) you will find the Museo de Mallorca, with the most comprehensive historical collection on the island – from Talayot culture to art of the 20th century. At Carrer Morei 7 you will find the unusual English bookshop Fine Books.

57__God's Roof
The cathedral terrace

There is no loftier position to look upon the city and over the sea. And what you find out high up on the broad roofs of the cathedral about the condition and history of this unique building from 1230 and its world of roof terraces, closed off for centuries, is definitely worth the climb up the narrow, stone, 215-step spiral staircase.

After around 70 steps, in front of the entrance to the bell tower, you reach a high room with the original organ pipes of the first organ of La Seu, and encounter centuries-old murals and mysterious characters inlaid in the walls. Further up in the bell tower, the massive wooden bell cage dominates with Mallorca's largest and heaviest bell, at 4,500 kilograms, which affects the whole statics of the tower due to its concentrated sonority. It is only rung on exceptional occasions, for example at the death or the selection of a pope, and once a year at Corpus Christi.

Finally, you reach the cathedral's large terraces, 44 metres above the marble floor of the nave – long dirty and inaccessible but now open to vsitors.

The dominant colour is the beige-red of the sandstone of the floors, walls, towers, spires, flowers and figures that ornament almost all of the walkways and balustrades. And the powerful, artfully designed flying buttresses between the nave and side aisles. Alongside the high stained-glass windows of the cathedral, whose glaring impression can of course only be truly appreciated from the inside, are represented above their exact position by huge photographs, with an explanation of their meaning and the names of the artists. Dominating everything is the huge rose window on the east façade, the coloured marvel of the cathedral, with a diameter of 12.55 metres, which captivates every viewer. And above the west portal you finally approach the patron saint of La Seu: Mary, with her arms spread out wide to heaven.

Address Catedral La Seu, Plaça Almoina, 07001 Palma de Mallorca, +34 (0)971 713133, www.catedraldemallorca.org | **Getting there** From Plaça de Reina via the large staircase past the Almudaina Palace | **Hours** May–Oct, reservations for the one-hour guided tour online: www.catedraldemallorca.org, groups up to 25 people, weekdays 6 tours 10am–1pm and 4–7pm, Sat 3 tours, meeting place: main side entrance on Plaça de la Seu | **Tip** You can also visit the roof terrace of the stock exchange where there are art exhibitions. There are also pretty roof terraces in the old town hotels Tres, Cuba and Sant Francesc.

58 The Grave of Ramon Llull

Where the father of the Catalonian language rests

Things really went bananas in this rather gloomy, but lavishly furnished church, the most important in Palma after the cathedral, on All Souls Day in the year 1490: out of the blue an argument broke out among Palma's aristocracy, which degenerated into a bloody massacre. Around 300 people lay dead in the pews and in front of the Portal of Sant Francesc after the service. The reasons for the feud remain a riddle to this day. Not a particularly glorious chapter for Palma's upper classes, and maybe this is why Saint George, the patron saint of the Mallorquin aristocracy, fights forever in an undecided battle with a dragon in the church in which Mallorca's greatest son, the philosopher and poet Ramon Llull (1232–1315), lies buried.

It isn't easy to find Llull's alabaster sarcophagus, in the church with its large colourful windows and the Gothic side chapel. The tomb diagonally behind the altar was designed by Francesc Sagrera in 1480, and is recessed above seven arches, which symbolise the seven arts and sciences of the Middle Ages, high up in a niche. You can see the effigy of this scholar and missionary, who is also considered the father of the Catalonian language due to his many philosophical and scientific texts, on his coffin.

In 1281, King James II had allowed the Franciscan Order to build the monastery and the church in the centre of the city. The centrepiece of the whole complex is the late-Gothic cloister from the 14th century with 115 intricate columns and pointed arches around the trapezium-shaped courtyard with palm trees and cypresses and a fountain. Today, the pupils of the Franciscan Catholic school, which is one of the best in the city, often spend their breaks in the cloister. The baroque façade of Sant Francesc, the imposing rose window and the portal with the group of sculptures by Francisco Herrera were created in the 17th century.

Address Plaça de Sant Francesc 7, 07001 Palma de Mallorca, +34 (0)971 712695 | Getting there The entrance to the church leads through the monastery seminary right of the church | Hours Mon – Sat 10am – 1.30pm & 2.15 – 5pm, Sun 9am – 1pm | Tip In front of the church is a memorial to the monk Junípero Serra (1713 – 1784) born in Petra, who left from Palma, Mallorca to evangelise in California and founded the city of San Francisco.

59___The House on the Rocks

Living in a risky location

At the end of the 18th century, when Palma was far from reaching as far as today's harbour for cruise ships, five close friends from the old town had the idea of buying a piece of land in front of the gates of the city in order to build a summer house. In this way they wanted to be able to leave the hectic city at any time and without complications, quickly in the evening or at the weekend, in order to swim and relax. They dreamed of their own small summer residence.

They bought the piece of land on top of the rocks for cheap in the place where the small boat port is today, opposite Club de Mar and near the harbour road Gabriel Roca. The new property was subdivided into five equal parts, and then the friends sorted out who should get which part. Simply and fairly, in the greatest of harmony.

They had their five small houses built and, as agreed, had one long veranda laid out in front of the houses, so that they could visit each other at any time and could walk from one to the other in an open atmosphere. After all, everything belonged to them collectively. Correspondingly, the houses on the plot had to be built pretty much in a line, and the last of the houses was so close to the cliffs that no fixed veranda could be installed. The five quickly found a solution: they built a balcony on struts in front of the house, sticking, so to speak, the veranda onto the cliffs. A temporary solution to this day. All of it of course strictly illegal, but romantic. On a stone staircase they built themselves, the friends could get to the water and throw themselves in within a few moments.

Private individuals still live in these houses. Some of them have been extended over the course of the years and converted into a hotel, which is now also exclusively private. The whole complex is called Portassa, the 'large door', just as the friends had wanted.

Address Avinguda de Joan Miró 105, 07015 Palma de Mallorca | Getting there Bus 1 to Porto Pi 8 (Club de Mar), or 102, 104, 106 or 107 to Gabriel Roca / Porto Pi | Tip A visit to the harbour with the cruise ships can be made from here (on Bus 1). You'll find a good view over the harbour from the small yard and park of the Fundació Amazonia, Avinguda de Joan Miró 101, which is right next to the 'house on the rocks'.

60__ The Inverted Church
Not a place to pray

You might not quite believe what your eyes are seeing on Plaça Porta de Santa Catalina. But there it is before you, a little church standing on its head, the spire artfully embedded in the ground, as if it were about to fall over at any moment. An object by American installation artist Dennis Oppenheim (1938–2011), whose specialities were large sculptures and room-filling pieces of metal, wood and stone. Oppenheim's sculptures are to be found in numerous metropolises around the world, including Palma, where the artist, who lived and worked in New York, often spent time.

The steel, aluminium and wood church standing on its head, with the title *Device to Root Out Evil*, is a replica of a piece that had its origins at the Venice Biennale in 1997 and now stands in Vancouver and Calgary in Canada among other places. The almost seven-metre-tall sculpture in Palma is a variation, composed slightly differently and only like the partner churches of the other cities in its general appearance. This airy painted aluminium and wood construction is as such a prototype. Badly defaced by graffiti, the church has recently been restored.

The Oppenheim chapel has come even more into its own since the Plaça Porta de Santa Catalina, which had degenerated into a grubby car park, was transformed into a charming traffic-calmed square with another object worth seeing: two huge granite pigeons, which seem to have landed among their many real conspecifics and started happily pecking away. And when the small upside-down chapel, lit from the inside in the evening, marks one side of the square in a shimmering slightly blue and the huge Santa Creu church illuminates the other, the square somehow feels like it spans epochs.

Dennis Oppenheim is represented on Mallorca with other spectacular works of art, for example an over-sized paintbrush – one of the highlights of the Es Baluard museum.

Address Plaça Porta de Santa Catalina, 07012 Palma de Mallorca | Getting there From Passeig des Born through Carrer de Sant Feliu and Can Sales or a few steps from the southern end of Passeig Mallorca | Tip If you fancy watching international films in their original language (German or English), the art house cinema Cine Ciutat (Carrer Emperadriu Eugènia 6), part of the S'Escorxador cultural centre in the old municipal slaughterhouse, is the place for you.

61 Joan Miró's Studio

This setting will make you want to be an artist

When Joan Miró signed over parts of his property in Cala Major to the city of Palma and formed a foundation in 1981, he wanted to ensure that his house and studio, and thus his permanently installed work, didn't fall victim, like so much on the island, to building speculation, bulldozers and the encroaching high-rises.

The painter, graphic designer and sculptor, who was born in Barcelona in 1893 and died aged 90 in Palma, always had a strong bond with Mallorca. His family on his mother's side came from the island, and his wife Pilar, whom he married in 1929, came from Sóller. From 1956, Miró lived and worked, after long stays in Barcelona and Paris, on the island. He had his friend and architect Josep Lluís Sert build the large Son Boter studio, in which epochal works were created over the course of decades. This can now be seen in its original working set up and is sure to make your artist heart beat a little faster.

As an aside: the master's work clothes still hang on the parapet of the gallery to the far left. Miró's home on a slope above the studio, a converted finca surrounded by cypresses, houses further studio rooms in the lower floor, whose walls were partially painted by the artist himself and which are furnished with objects of all kinds. After Miró's death, his wife and the foundation had the architect Rafael Moneo construct a museum building with sculpture garden and water roof, which is now the foundation's main office and represents the centrepiece of the Miró Fundació, with constantly changing exhibits. In total the foundation has over 2,500 exhibits by the artist, whose work is made up of oil paintings, sculptures, ceramics, collages and drawings. The lettering 'España', which adorns the yellow-black-red logo of the 1982 football World Cup and is today the symbol of the Spanish tourist office, enjoys a huge level of recognition.

Address Fundació Pilar i Joan Miró a Mallorca, Carrer Saridakis 29, 07015 Palma de Mallorca, +34 (0)971 701420, www.miro.palmademallorca.es | **Getting there** Bus 3 or 46 from the city centre | **Hours** 16 May–15 Sept Tue–Sat 10am–7pm, Sun & holidays 10am–3pm; 16 Sept–15 May Tue–Sat 10am–6pm, Sun & holidays 10am–3pm | **Tip** Below the cathedral in Parc de la Mar is a huge wall ceramic by Miró. The 3.50-metre-tall and 12-metre-wide tiled wall was made in 1983, shortly before the artist's death.

62 The Maritime Exchange

Culture in Palma's most prestigious room

The building is among the most magnificent that the old trading city of Palma has to offer. And yet many visitors walk straight past it, partly because for years there was no admission to the public. This has now changed: at least when the maritime exchange, radically restored in recent years, awaits with changing exhibitions of contemporary art. The great hall – essentially the whole building is one single enclosed space – in which there have also been legendary carnival parties in past decades that insiders still gush over today, gives the exhibited pieces a unique flair, also due to the light that streams in through the large windows.

The former produce and money exchange is made of Santanyí stone and looks almost like a cathedral in the Catalan Gothic style from the outside, with its six mighty ogive windows, the eight smaller and larger towers, the battlements and the patron saints for the individual merchant classes. It was built as an assembly hall for Palma's merchants between 1426 and 1447 by the Mallorquin star architect and builder Guillem Sagrera, who was also significantly involved in the building of the cathedral. After all, Palma had active trading relationships with around two dozen countries at the start of the 15th century, that continued until the 18th century. Later, during the War of Independence, the building was used as a store for goods and guns.

The ostentatious maritime trade building, which has a guardian angel watching over its entrance, also symbolises the prosperity and wealth of Palma and Mallorca in this period. According to oral tradition, during a visit in the 16th century Holy Roman Emperor Charles V thought Palma's Sa Llotja was a cathedral. The building spans a rectangle measuring 46 metres by 28 metres. Inside, in three naves, six slender, spiralling columns, which fan out upwards like palm trees, bear the mighty dome.

Address La Llotja, Plaça Llotja 5, am Passeig de Sagrera, 07012 Palma de Mallorca, +34 (0)971 711705 | Getting there From Passeig des Born on the Carrer del Apuntadores and Carrer Sant Juan | Hours During exhibitions Tue–Sat 11am–2pm & 5–9pm (in winter to 8pm), Sun 11am–1pm, otherwise make sure you take a look inside through the large windows | Tip In the immediate vicinity is the Consolat de Mar, the building of the maritime trade court from the 17th century. In front of it stands a completely white memorial to the author Rubén Darío (1867–1916).

63__Marivent

The royal garden of the summer residence

The citizens of Palma, especially those of Cala Major, were pretty annoyed that they were never allowed to see behind the high, thick walls of the gardens of the Marivent palace, the summer residence of the Spanish royal family, located on a rocky elevation by the sea. Not for voyeuristic reasons, but more because of the beautiful botanical park, which had remained closed to subjects for decades. A painstaking negotiation between the government of the Balearic Islands and the Spanish royal family led to an agreement that now ensures that around a third of the total grounds, the Mediterranean front garden of the palace, is open to visitors. After all, in the 1970s the government ceded use of the huge plot of 32,000 square metres with park and palace – which was built in 1925 by Ioannes Saridakis, an Egyptian-Greek engineer, artist and patron – to the Spanish royal family. They moved in in 1975, and have since spent their summers here, occasionally receiving monarchs and heads of states.

In May 2017, the time had finally come for the royal garden to open the large gate on Avinguda de Joan Miró to the public – with no entrance fee. Most visitors had imagined the more than 9,000-square-metre plot to be bigger, but what the park had to offer in quality was compensation enough. Bougainvilleas, roses and lilies, date palms and cypresses, artfully cut hedges and striking arrangements of flowers, fountains and shady arbours and a multitude of attractive green spaces tended by numerous gardeners. And amongst all of this, the real highlight of the garden: 12 bronze sculptures by Joan Miró, which the heirs of the artist, who lived only a few kilometres inland, donated to the royal garden.

An iron fence now divides the public from the private garden of the royal family. When the family is in residence, the park stays completely closed to their subjects.

Address Jardins de Marivent, Avinguda de Joan Miró 229, 07015 Palma de Mallorca | **Getting there** Bus 4 or 46 to Joan Miró Marivent | **Hours** Daily summer: 9am–8pm; winter: 9am–4.30pm; closed 15 July–15 Sept and Easter week | **Tip** A visit to La Almudaina royal palace in the city centre with the wonderful throne room is recommended. Furthermore, the new Cala Nova harbour with restaurant and bar in Cala Major invites you to linger a while.

64 Museu dels Molins
On the trail of the island's emblem

There are over 1,000 windmills in greater Palma. Most of them, like those you see in their dozens around the airport, when you glide down onto the island, once powered water pumps, essential for the barren island. There are also a few dozen windmills that used to be flour mills. These are larger and bulkier and are mostly not located on the plains, but rather on exposed windy places, such as above the harbour in the district of El Jonquet, which was once a little fishing village just outside the gates of the city. These mills date back to the early 15th century, while most of the mills you encounter on the island and those that have become Mallorca's emblem, date back to the 17th and 18th centuries.

The base of the Mallorquin windmill for flour production was a hefty square or round stonework construction, known as a 'cintell', in which the grain was stored, but also where the miller sometimes lived. The roughly eight-metre-tall cylindrical tower with a diameter of 4.5 metres and walls over a metre thick stood on top of the Cintell.

A staircase led through the inside of the mill up to under the roof, on which the wind paddles, mostly wooden, were attached. These were connected with the millstone underneath it by a shaft. Most mill wheels were made up of six arms, which were woven like a spider's web with struts. There are five of these windmills right by the sea along the harbour.

Thanks to private initiatives and the city of Palma, for some years these cultural memorials have been in reasonable condition again and have become a trademark of the evermore attractive residential district of El Jonquet. For a long time these mills had fallen into disrepair or were used for other purposes, for example as discotheques. The small museum in d'en Garleta mill, which opened in 2005, vividly presents the history of Mallorca's mills.

Address Carrer del Molí d'en Garleta 14, 07013 Palma de Mallorca, +34 (0)676 838477 |
Getting there On foot from Avinguda d'Argentina at Plaça de la Feixina turn into
Carrer de Sant Magi, then left onto Carrer dels Molins de Migjorn | Hours Tue & Thu
10.30am – 12.30pm | Tip Four more old mills, of which only the first still has a six-armed
wind wheel, can be viewed a few streets further into the city on Carrer de l'Indústria, corner
of Carrer del Comte de Barcelona.

65__ The Nativity Scene
3,000 figures and things from all walks of life

This nativity scene is unique. If you come in from the terrace, you'll find it just inside the entrance to the Museu Palau March, behind glass and spread over three rooms. The Museu Palau March is the former family home of the banker Juan March, built between 1939 and 1945 in the style of an Italian Baroque palace and is not far from the cathedral. Today, it is the headquarters of the Bartolomé March Servera foundation.

There are 3,000 intricate, Capodimonte porcelain figures and objects modelled in great detail, but also wax figures dressed in the finest silk fabrics, decorated and coloured, real right down to the eyelashes. They populate the oriental fantasy world based on the birth of Jesus in such a manner that the actual manger with the holy child is almost upstaged. This goes far beyond a conventional nativity scene. It is therefore only right that it can be admired all year round.

The three wise men, the kings of Orient, appear to be riding towards the manger from all the provinces of the East, accompanied by bands of musicians and huge entourages, dressed in their respective national costumes, with lots of decoration, worked out to the smallest detail. There are also dozens of everyday scenes, which show the lives of simple people: busy people on market squares, butchers slaughtering, bakers and bread, women cooking, mothers breastfeeding, fishmongers, drinking sessions, all with elaborate expressions and gestures. Everyday Neapolitan stories. A 'world theatre in miniature' the *FAZ* newspaper called it, a spectacle that transcends the classes.

Neapolitan nativity scenes were very popular toys in the royal courts and aristocratic circles of the 18th century. They became bestsellers 'made in Napoli'. Bartolomé March, one of Juan March's sons, bought and put together one of the prettiest mangers of its kind, modelled by renowned artists of the time.

Address Museu Palau March, Palau Reial 18, 07001 Palma de Mallorca | **Getting there** From Plaça de la Reina via the Costa de la Seu steps | **Hours** Apr–Oct Mon–Fri 10am–6.30pm, Nov–Mar Mon–Fri 10am–5pm, Sat 10am–2pm | **Tip** You must take a look at the excellent music room in Palau March with walls painted by the most famous Catalonian muralist Josep Maria Sert (1876–1945). Museu Fundació Juan March in the Sant Miquel 11 city palace is also worth a visit.

66__Pere Garau Market

Lively hustle and bustle away from the tourists

On this market you will encounter a Palma that hardly feels like the Mediterranean metropolis. It is more like visiting a north African city. This is where real life plays out, at least on market days, when shopping becomes a social experience. Pere Garau is located beyond Plaça d'Espanya, and for that fact alone foreigners only extremely rarely stumble upon it. What is for sale at this multicultural market place is not only worth looking at, but also worth taking home with you. The range of goods on offer impresses with fair prices and especially its quality. This is where the housewives of Palma do their shopping, and many restaurateurs stop off here too.

Palma's oldest market awaits with permanent market stalls in one large hall. Long fresh meat and fish counters with everything you could imagine and more. Here you would never dream that parts of the Mediterranean are overfished. Then there are sausage and ham stalls that will make your heart jump for joy. Iberian delicacies, finely cut, neatly packaged and handed over with a smile. Cheese stands, baked goods, blade sharpeners for keeping your knife sharp for cutting ham, stalls full of treats, where you can test and taste what is on display, and a lottery terminal – with so many epicurean and visual blessings, you might feel lucky about picking up the big prize.

Twice a week, on Tuesdays and Thursdays, there is also a large outdoor market on Pere Garau, dominated by fruit, vegetables, plants and gardening products, delivered direct from the Mallorquin farmers. And then there is the open-air animal market, which also happens twice a week. It takes some getting used to, but it's very popular among many Mallorquins. On Tuesdays and Saturdays you'll hear chirps, screeches, crows and bleats coming from the cages next to the large hall, crammed full of hundreds of chickens, birds, rabbits and sheep.

Address Plaça Pere Garau, 07007 Palma de Mallorca, +34 (0)971 244674 | Getting there
Coming from Plaça d'Espanya through Avinguda de Alejandro Rosselló, past El Corte
Inglés department store, into Carrer de Nuredduna or through Carrer d'Aragó and turn into
Carrer de Faust Morell | Hours Mon & Wed 6am–2.30pm, Tue, Thu & Fri 6am–3pm,
Sat 6am–4pm | Tip Other food markets in Palma: Mercat de l'Olivar (Plaça de l'Olivar),
fruit and vegetables: Santa Catalina (Plaça Navegació), fish: Llotja del Peix (Es Moll de
Pescadores, Mon–Sat 7am–2pm).

67 Santa Clara Convent

Ice cream and cake through the hatch

They are not allowed to leave the convent grounds, they live almost self-sufficiently and hardly ever show themselves in public, except during the Christmas period, when they sell homemade Christmas decorations, cake and almond or chocolate creations from behind a large grate in an old convent building. You shouldn't speak to the sisters of the Franciscan Order of Saint Claire either. At most you can offer an 'Avemaria Purísima' ('Hail Mary'). The code forbids the sisters, who live in strict seclusion beyond all the din of the city, from saying any more.

The Convento de Santa Clara, one of the oldest convents in Palma, and founded in 1256, is hidden in the tangle of alleyways of the old town, but is well worth a visit. What you experience there, you won't find anywhere else on the island. Discretion is a condition, calm and restraint are a matter of course.

Normally you won't catch sight of a nun when you cross the courtyard and enter the side wing of the building, with its door open during the day signalling that you are absolutely welcome. That's because this is the convent's outlet, the salesroom for homemade confectionery and ice cream specialities. A list of products and prices hangs on the door.

Inside there is a hatch, known as a 'torno', which is recessed within a white tiled rectangle, surrounded by a coloured ornamented band, visible through an open wooden door, secured by a chain. If you press the bell on the wall, also framed by tiles, a mysterious voice asks what it is you want. You answer in a low voice, place your order, and wait for whatever is coming. A little later the hatch swivels around, and out comes your order right in front of you. Then you place the payment, exact or rounded up, in the hatch, which is turned again as if by magic and then closes again. Goods in return for trust. A matter of course in Santa Clara.

Address Convento de Santa Clara, Carrer de Can Fonollar 2, 07001 Palma de Mallorca, +34 (0)971 710061 | Getting there Behind the cathedral in Carrer de Sant Bernat, further into Carrer de la Puresa to the end then right into Carrer de Santa Clara | Hours Daily 9am–12.30pm & 4.15–6.45pm | Tip It's also worth taking a look at the convent church, in which the nuns pray, separated from visitors by a grille. The Augustine Santa Magdalena convent is also worth seeing (Plaça de Santa Magdalena 4, daily 9.30am–12.30pm & 4.15–5.30pm).

68__Santa Creu Church

Palma's time-honoured house of God

While probably Palma's oldest church, Santa Creu ('The holy cross') receives far less attention than the cathedral or the great churches in the upper part of the Old Town. However, it is definitely worth a visit. What makes Santa Creu (or Spanish: Santa Cruz) special is that it consists of two churches really.

In the 13th century, the San Lorenzo chapel was built in the Early Gothic style on the foundations of a Moorish temple in the old seafarers' quarter high above the harbour. Today, this subterranean crypt with its freestanding columns lies beneath the chancel of the main church, as over the centuries Santa Creu was redesigned repeatedly.

With the congregation growing, the new, much larger church was erected above the chapel, and work on it would continue from the 15th century onwards. It was only in the 18th century that Santa Creu was finally completed, with a rebuilt main doorway and a splendid high altar, which is why the bell tower and the crypt of Saint Llorenc (San Lorenzo chapel) represent the oldest parts of the building today. The crypt, which has its own street entrance, is only opened up for Sunday Mass.

The ceiling of the main church consists of an imposing Gothic groin vault resting on octagonal pillars, while the walls are adorned with numerous Baroque and Gothic wooden panels.

Santa Creu boasts an impressive Baroque organ built by master organ builder Damià Caimari in the mid-18th century. In 2018, the organ was newly consecrated after seven years of restauration. The church also houses a museum with numerous sacred art exhibits from the island, including a silver processional cross from the Valldemossa charterhouse and a centuries old tabernacle. The statue occupying pride of place above the entrance on the northern façade represents Saint Helena of Constantinople.

Address Iglesia Santa Creu, Carrer Sant Llorenc 1, 07012 Palma de Mallorca; Catholic parish office: Carrer Forn de l'Olivera 5, +34 (0)971 264551 | **Getting there** The church is in the lower old town on Plaça Porta de Santa Catalina close to the museum Es Baluard. | **Hours** Mon, Tue, Thu & Fri 11am–12.30pm; Sun noon, Mass in German in the crypt | **Tip** Don't miss a look at the bright red, 3.70-metre-tall metal sculpture *Palma* by Mallorquin artist Josep Llambías, situated between the city wall and the harbour, next to Sa Llotja. *Palma* has become something of a symbol for the city.

69___The Sundial

Telling the time in a different way

It is often claimed that Mallorca has the highest density of sundials in the whole of Europe. Experts even speak of over 700 small and large works of this kind, spread across the whole island, right up into the villages of the Tramuntana mountain range. They can be found in monasteries, churches, palaces and estates, in parks and gardens, in small and large designs, vertical and horizontal to the sun, sometimes painted on limestone, but also engraved in stone. In the centre of all the installations is always the iron shadow stick, technically speaking called a 'gnomon'. Of course, if the sun is not shining, you can't read the time, but happily the sun shines a lot on Mallorca. If the sundial's pointer casts its shadow on the 12, it is noon.

Most of the sundials on Mallorca are from the 17th and 18th centuries, but there are also many newer specimens, which have more of a decorative character than the aspiration to be taken seriously as chronometers.

In Palma alone there are around a dozen public, imposing installations, some of which have told the time for decades, but only for those who can read them: very few people actually know how sundials really work. This used to be different. Over the centuries sundials defined the daily routine of islanders, people read the time in this clever, but natural way, based on the state of the sun.

One of the most impressive sundials in Palma, which is also one that many visitors stroll past every day, is the example that stands on Avinguda Gabriel Roca below the mills of Es Jonquet. You can also find other sundials very close by. Diagonally opposite at the harbour for example, where the colourful fishing nets are always laid out to dry, or at the beginning of Feixina park. Finally there is a large, poured concrete sundial with a shadow stick as thick as an anchor on the pier of the old shipyard harbour.

ANY MCMLXXXVI

HORES DE POSTES

HORES DE SORTIDES

Address Avinguda de Gabriel Roca by the mills of Es Jonquet, 07012 Palma de Mallorca | **Getting there** In the extension of Passeig de Sagrera past Es Baluard museum | **Tip** Mallorca's most unusual sundial is in Santuari de Lluc monastery, the only known multiple sundial, that shows the Central European, the Babylonian and the canonical time simultaneously on different clock faces.

70__The Templar Signets
Symbols from a time long ago

The order, which was originally called the 'Poor Fellow-Soldiers of Christ and of the Temple of Solomon', was founded following the first crusades (1096–1099) and the capture of Jerusalem in 1118 near the Temple of Solomon. Originally intended as guards to protect pilgrims and Christian sites in hostile Palestine, the Knights Templar grew to be one of the most mysterious alliances in the Middle Ages, were mandated by the Pope and became a fifth column of the Vatican. The troops comprised over 15,000 men at times, who were armed to the hilt. They saw themselves as the link between religion and chivalry, and expanded into Europe, thus also into Spain. Mallorca was one of the Templar Order's strongholds.

The Templars entered the battle for the reconquest of the south from the 800-year-long rule of the Moors in 1158 as an order of knights of the Spanish Reconquista. The Templar monks with the red cross on their shoulders, said to be a reminder of the passion of Jesus, fought loyally at the side of James I of Aragón. After the surrender of the Emirs in 1229 and the subordination of Mallorca under Christian domination, the Templars were rewarded with a quarter of all conquests. They owned around 400 houses and 50 workshops in Palma alone. El Temple on Plaça de Temple in the district of Calatrava, built around 1230 on a Muslim fortress, was their centre of power and there are still visible signs today. The remains of the Templar castle and the Templar church are visible, but are barely mentioned in the travel guides.

The persecution of the Templars all throughout Europe began in 1308. The Pope and secular rulers handed the knights, who had become increasingly powerful and could no longer be controlled, over to the Inquisition for heresy and high treason. A few years later, the order was completely crushed and the Templar assets on Mallorca were seized by James II.

Address Carrer del Temple 9, 07001 Palma de Mallorca | Getting there From Sant Francesc church through Carrer Ramón Llull in the Carrer del Temple or coming from the end of Parc de la Mar through Carrer de la Porta de Mar | Hours The church's vestibule with a notice board is usually open for one hour from noon. In order to get into the church, you have to ring the bell at the door on the left and ask for the door to be opened. | Tip The altarpiece with Saint Bernard of Clairvaux, one of the spiritual fathers of the Templar, which hung for a long time in the Templar church, can now be seen in Museu de Mallorca.

71 The Town Hall Library

A temple to reading in the old town

For newcomers or tourists, this is a real insider tip among all the highly visible historical buildings the city has to offer. The library, in its wood-panelled setting, is the ideal place for those wanting to escape the tourist stress of the old town and withdraw for a rest, and perhaps read a book or a newspaper, of which there is an international selection to peruse.

In order to get to the library at the end of the large town hall chamber, you pass some metre-tall modelled figures of Mallorquin farmers; their aristocratic pendants stand one building on in the seat of the Insular Council.

The library, opened in 1935, was intended to be an example, signalling the advent of education that should be open and accessible to every citizen. At least that's how the socialists and liberal spirits who governed during the Spanish Republic saw it. It was also intended to serve to make education, which was frequently reserved for the upper class alone, accessible to the illiterate, whose numbers were still very high at the time. Libraries and bookshops mushroomed right across the country in this period.

The library in Palma was also in operation during the era of fascist rule. But after the end of the Franco dictatorship it flourished again in a renewed intellectual environment. In addition, there is also Palma's large city archives with a chronicle of the history and events from 1206 to this day.

The impressive mid-17th-century town hall bears an artfully ornate wooden roof, jutting far out over the frontage. The three-storey façade symbolises the transition from Mannerism to Baroque. The large clock 'En Figuera' mounted above the portal, is one of the first of its kind in Spain, and is especially impressive. The recessed bench between the entrances to the town hall is a great place to watch the goings-on on Plaça de Cort.

Address Biblioteca Municipal de Cort, Plaça de Cort 1, 07001 Palma de Mallorca, +34 (0)971 225962 | Getting there From Passeig des Born on foot through Carrer Constitició or from Plaça de la Reina through Carrer Conquistador | Hours Sat 9am–1pm | Tip Worth seeing is the centuries-old olive tree that stands on the town hall square, now traffic-calmed. To the right of the town hall is the Palau del Consell, a neo-Gothic building with little towers and garlands, reminiscent of a fairytale castle, which is the seat of the Consell de Mallorca, the Insular Council.

72__ The Wind Pyramid

Really stand in the wind

You always drive, stroll or cycle past it if you're out and about on the El Molinar promenade: the strange, six-sided structure that rises steeply up towards the sky with the bird sculpture on its apex and the base tiled with colourful mosaics that can be reached up four steps. Some kind of symbolic obelisk? A special lighthouse for seafarers? An orientation point for hydrographic surveying? A work of art?

The former fishing village of El Molinar – which now belongs to the city of Palma and has the 28 grain windmills to thank for its name, of which three are still standing today after the rest were demolished in the 1970s and 1980s – was also furnished with a brand new promenade during this period. It's east of Clubs Marítimo de Levante, Mallorca's first sports' boat harbour, which was created back at the beginning of the century. This idiosyncratic stone structure was built in the bay of El Molinar, centrally, on a concrete base pushed forward towards the sea, as part of the fundamental redesign of the promenade that was carried out back then: a kind of pyramid with a function. Now you could see from far off where the wind was blowing from: by looking at a bird on the top that turns in the wind. There had never been anything like it.

But the cock became jammed years ago and stopped turning. No matter how much the storm raged on the sea, the bird, or as the people in El Molinar called it, the 'Corb Mari', the cormorant, was rusted, worn out by the weather. In 2019, the wind pyramid was finally radically restored, in particular a new bird sculpture, with a wingspan of two-and-a-half metres, was added. Lighter and made of aluminium, fixed to a five-and-a-half-metre-tall stainless steel bar. And at night lit up by LED lamps. The former emblem of El Molinar, the mill, has definitely given way to the distinctive hexagonal wind pyramid as the symbol of the quarter.

Address Carrer del Vicari Joaquim Fuster 227, 07007 Palma de Mallorca | Getting there From Palma take the Ma-19 to El Molinar, on the roundabout onto Carrer de Llucmajor, keep right and turn onto Carrer de Josep Amengual to the beach | Hours Always accessible | Tip El Molinar has its own theatre with 222 seats, Teatre del Mar at Carrer de Llucmajor 90. It is not far to the impressive aquarium in Can Pastilla (Carrer Manuela de los Herreros i Serà 21).

73__ Torre de Porto Pi
The oldest lighthouse in the Mediterranean

It is considered fairly certain that the lower square stone tower of Torre de Porto Pi with the crenellations and battlements is from the period of Moorish rule on Mallorca. After all, it was mentioned in a document in 1290 and was converted into a lighthouse in 1369 at the behest of James II. At this time, however, the tower was still offset sideways in the location of the historic Sant Carles fortress today. Torre de Porto Pi corresponds with its partner tower Torre de Paraires on the other side of the harbour to the north. The harbour entrance could be blocked at will using a chain hung between the two towers.

With the construction of the fortress in 1613, the tower was shifted to its current position in the harbour, raised to a 40-metre-tall lighthouse and furnished with 12 oil lamps as signal lights. In the 18th century the lamp dome, with its current 1,000-watt-strong halogen lamps, was completely glazed. Today, the lighthouse, which is still in service, is fully automated, and its signals can be seen for 20 sea miles.

And the port, one of the largest in the western Mediterranean, is always very busy. Eight cruise ships can dock at the port terminal at the same time, annually around 1.6 million passengers come ashore here in order to explore Palma. This area is also still a trading and military port.

Although Torre de Porto Pi appears unapproachable and hard to access to most people due to its location and function, since 2004 it has housed a small museum, that can be viewed on three days in the week by appointment. On display in a permanent exhibition are maritime signals, nautical measuring instruments, lighting systems, maps and all sorts of objects related to the history of lighthouses on the Balearics. If you're feeling particularly energetic you can also climb up another 127 steps to the lantern house of the glazed beacon dome.

Address Far de Porto Pi, Carretera Arsenal 3E, 07015 Palma de Mallorca | Getting there
On the Avinguda de Gabriel Roca towards Cala Major, on the roundabout Porto Pi onto
Carretera Dic de l'Oest, after 200 metres left into Carretera Arsenal | Hours Lighthouse
museum: Mon, Wed, Fri 10am – 1.30pm, booking by telephone or e-mail essential on
+34 (0)971 402175 or +34 (0)971 228155 or fardeportopi@portsdebalears.com | Tip
At the exit of the yacht harbour at the end of Carrer del Moll, behind the tiny Plaça de
Jardins de Sant Telm, is the small mariners' chapel of the same name, where services are
held on Sunday mornings.

74_ The Wickerwork Paradise

Mimbrería Vidal is a shop in a class of its own

A shop like this is hard to find. In fact, there can only be one of its kind on Mallorca – here, deep in the old town of Palma where you can find an astonishing number of small specialty stores.

Mimbrería Vidal is a shop that stocks almost anything you can think of to do with hemp, raffia, palm leaves or sisal. A shop far from all the hustle and bustle, that has been run by the same family for over 80 years. Once, however, the Corderia was blessed with a whole series of basket makers, one of the oldest handicrafts on Mallorca and a skill that was passed on from generation to generation.

Mimbrería Vidal, run by a father and son team, is one of the last weaving workshops of its kind on the island. Most of the goods are produced in north-east Mallorca, especially in the region of Artà. Here the women are still masters of Palmito weaving, using the branches of the dwarf palm. That's why you always get real handicraft for your money here in Mimbrería Vidal. This is also what makes it an indispensable address for the Mallorquins.

The shop is full of hundreds of these woven bags, hanging everywhere, so you always have the feeling it's time to rush off to the beach. But these bags, made in all sizes and in various qualities, actually serve the Mallorquins in many ways: for shopping at the market, as storage space, and if there's nowhere else, infants have been known to sleep in one of these huge containers. In Mimbrería Vidal you can buy almost everything made of wickerwork. Shopping and handbags, washing baskets, fruit and wastepaper baskets, lampshades, carpets, hammocks and hats. Mainly in light colours, beige and brown, but also adorned with flashy accents on request. Hundreds of baskets hang in the completely overfilled shop, right up to the roof, and lots of chairs, as one of the specialities of the family business are woven chair constructions, seat tops and backrests, which are still produced on site by father and son themselves.

Address Mimbrería Vidal, Carrer de la Correria 13, 07002 Palma de Mallorca, +34 (0)971 711243 | Getting there On foot from Plaça Major or Santa Eulalia to Plaça Coll, from which Correria forks off | Hours Mon–Fri 9.30am–1.30pm & 4.30–8pm | Tip It's worth taking a look into the courtyard of the nearby 18th-century city palace of Marqués de Vivot at Carrer de Can Savellà 4.

75 Ermita de Bonany

A church as an event

Once you reach the 317-metre-high Puig de Bonany, the stairs up to the church seem almost majestic. Past a neat garden, you reach the church portal through an archway with colourful tiles on the left and an espalier of palms and cypresses. Entering the church becomes an event. It smells of incense and herbs, meditative music sounds from discreet speakers, along with choral music and hymns. You become reflective, sit down, listen, whisper. On the left a small altar, a Bethlehem grotto, but more expressive, also more kitsch and playful than the one on the holy mount of Randa. Angels, stars, the holy family in a lush landscape. Right and left of the manger you look through magnifying bull's-eye windows, to gain a three-dimensional sense of the nativity landscape, into caves and upon hills, the details drawn right up close to you. Smells and sounds continue to accompany you if you round the altar and step in front of the virgin of Bonany. 'Bonany' basically means 'good year'.

The slightly strange looking, rather rotund Madonna from the 8th century owes her name to a 'miracle' from the 17th century. After a devastatingly dry period, which wiped out the harvest and the livestock, the people's prayers to this Madonna are supposed to have brought the long-yearned-for rain and saved cattle and harvest. Colourful tile pictures inlaid in the archway below the church recall the events of those days.

Although the Ermita de Nostra Senyora de la Bonany between Petra, Villafranca de Bonany and Sant Joan is visible from afar, enthroned on the peak of the mountain, relatively few tourists in cars find their way up here via the narrow road, though it's more popular among bikers, who see the Puig de Bonany as a physical challenge and don't come for the cultural highlights. But the journey up to the Puig really is an experience and the view from up there is quite breathtaking.

Address 07520 Petra | **Getting there** From Petra on the Ma-3220 towards Sant Joan, exit at kilometre 4 | **Hours** During daylight | **Tip** Really cheap spartan furnished rooms of the old hermitage are let out in the old monastery (+34 (0)971 561101). A solid stone cross on the road near the church pays memory to the last sermon that Junípero Serra gave here before he set off to begin his missionary work in the New World.

76_Junípero Serra's Home

The founder of San Francisco came from Mallorca

If you were to suggest that the Californian metropolises of San Francisco, San Diego and Santa Clara had a direct link to the small, 3,000-person Mallorquin village of Petra, there would be a lot of doubters. But the claim is true. And there are visible signs to support this in Petra.

"The Franciscan monk Junipero Serra (1713–1784) was born here. He is best known for establishing 21 missions beginning in 1749 in today's Mexico and 1776 in Southern California, many of which are now cities that still bear their Spanish names, including Santa Barbara, Los Angeles, and San Jose. But more still: Junípero Serra is understood to have founded San Francisco in 1776, which is also the date of the United States' Declaration of Independence. Today, a statue of him stands in the United States Capitol's National Statuary Hall, amongst the greatest of American heroes. This is something people are particularly proud of in Petra. But also that Junípero Serra, who died in California in 1784 and was also buried there, was beatified by Pope John Paul II in 1988. As an aside: Junípero Serra, the son of a simple farmer, is also said to have introduced wine growing to California. Wine growing also assures the livelihoods of many people in Petra.

Not far from the tiny, whitewashed birthplace of the small town's greatest son, which is in Barracar Alt, the oldest part of the town, is a museum, built in 1959, that documents the monk's missionary work. In the 17th-century Sant Pere church, you can still see the Gothic font over which the young Serra was held, and on the wall hangs a large commemorative plaque. He went to school in the Convent de Sant Bernardí. His memorial stands on Plaça del Padre Serra. In Carrer Fra Junípera you will come across colourful tile pictures that show stations of the exciting life story of the monk from Petra, who entered the Franciscan Order at just 16 years old.

Address Casa Natal i Museu Junipero Serra, Carrer Barracar Alt 6 – 8, 07520 Petra, +34 (0)971 561149 | **Getting there** Petra is on the main road Ma-3320 from Manacor in the direction of Inca | **Hours** The opening times are irregular. If the museum is closed, a panel will tell you where you can collect the key. | **Tip** Next to the San Pere church is a large monument in honour of female Mallorquin farmers.

77__The Pilgrim's Path
Meditative trip to the Black Madonna

'Lluc by foot' is a dictum on Mallorca, meaning there is barely a family on the island from which at least one member has not made a pilgrimage to Lluc monastery. The monastery, high up in the Tramuntana mountain range, is after all the spiritual centre of the island. A pilgrimage to Lluc in honour of the Black Madonna is part of the repertoire of every devout Mallorquin. In the summer they hike through the Tramuntana mountain range in their hundreds, singing happily, doing penance, in order to pay homage to the Mare de Déu de Lluc and afterwards to stop for something to eat in the monastery restaurant or to picnic on one of the large barbecue sites. Many pilgrims also spend the night in one of the monastery's plain guest rooms. Not all too difficult, but especially appealing is the almost 14-kilometre-long historic pilgrim's path from Pollença to Lluc, which begins near the old Roman bridge, Pont Romà. You need a good four-and-a-half hours for this classic pilgrim's path to the monastery at around 500 metres above sea level, but it is quite manageable – more like an exclusive walk through wonderful landscape. You cross the Puig Tomir and mountain passes and streams, pass by orange groves and hike through holm oak forests.

People have made pilgrimages to the Black Madonna or, as she is called by the Mallorquins, Sa Moreneta, the 'small black one' since the Reconquista. In 1229, the shepherd boy Lluc is said to have found the statue in the place where the monastery stands today and to have brought it to the priest of Escora church. But the Madonna disappeared overnight, back to its original place. After this mysterious spectacle had been repeated several times, it was understood to be a sign from the Lord and ultimately a small chapel was built at the place the Black Madonna was found, the laying of the foundations for the Lluc monastery.

Address Long-distance trail 221 at Pont Roma, 07460 Pollença | **Getting there** On the Ma-13 past Sa Pobla and then on the Ma-2200 to Pollença | **Hours** Lluc monastery: daily 10am–6pm | **Tip** Since 2018, Lluc monastery is now the official starting point of the Way of Saint James from Mallorca to Santiago de Compostela, replacing Sant Honorat monastery on Randa's holy mount.

78 The Roman Bridge

When the stream becomes a raging torrent

The exact dating of the Pont Roma, the old 'Roman bridge' on the northern city outskirts of Pollença is uncertain, but it probably dates from the 5th century, just like the old Roman settlement of Pollentia in front of the gates of the old town of Alcúdia. After the assault on the Balearic Islands and the violent plundering and destruction of Pollentia by the Gauls and Vandals, and the assimilation of the islands into the kingdom of the Vandals, the survivors of the massacre fled inland and settled further north beyond the protective river, in today's Pollença, which they named after their old capital. They built the stone bridge over Torrent de Sant Jordi, which is otherwise very hard to cross. It almost dries out in summer, but can become a raging torrent in autumn and winter.

Right into the 20th century, Pont Roma was the only place at which the torrent could be crossed during flooding in order to reach the city. Today the the bridge, meanwhile a Unesco World Heritage Site, is still frequented by local inhabitants on the way into the old town. Crossing it always gives one a deep connection to the long history of its existence.

The walk up the 365 natural stone steps – one for each day of the year – lined by cypresses, pines and cacti, flanked by 14 three-metre-high crosses, up the 170-metre-high Puig de Calvari, is also a must for every visitor to Pollença. The view of the city, with the ochre-coloured roofs of the houses, the Puig de Santa Maria opposite, the broad fruit gardens along the Torrent de Sant Jordi with the Pont Roma and over the plains to the sea with the bays of Pollença and Alcúdia from the wide terrace, is captivating. The Puig de Calvari has been venerated since the middle of the 13th century, when, as the chronicles say, castaways from Cala Sant Vincenç erected a cross high up here above the settlement by way of thanks for their rescue.

Address Carrer del Pont Roma, 07460 Pollença | Getting there On the Ma-13 past Sa Pobla and then on the Ma-2200 to Pollença, on the Ma-10 north of the city onto Camí de Ternelles | Hours Always accessible | Tip Font de Gall, the 'cockerel fountain' from 1827, on Carrer de Joan Mas just behind Plaça Major and the Santa Maria dels Àngels church is worth a visit. It is said that those who wish for something in the presence of the black cockerel can assume that it will be fulfilled.

79_Puig de Monti-Sión

Take a pilgrimage and ask for mercy

It is worth driving up here even after the onset of darkness. Admittedly, you will have to allow a bit of extra time for the drive up the narrow road on the 248-metre-tall Puig de Monti-Sión. But the restaurant with Mallorquin cuisine (reservations on +34 (0)971 647185) is compensation enough as well as the atmosphere, which is created by the varied lighting of the complex. But the drive by daylight offers more. Then the Way of the Cross and the corresponding Stations from the Middle Ages can be seen on both sides of the road, as well as seven Gothic columns, representing each of the Holy Mary's Seven Joys and Seven Sorrows.'

The Monti-Sión monastery, consecrated to the Holy Mother of Mount Zion, is an oasis of peace during the week. Via an expansive staircase, past a historic draw well, you reach the courtyard with its impressive cloister. The small church, the nucleus of the entire monastery complex, was built around 1500. For more than 300 years, from the middle of the 16th century, the monastery housed a theological school, later one of the oldest and most important schools of grammar and Latin on the island, which qualified pupils to study in Palma, but it was closed in 1835 due to political changes.

Though the Santuari de Monti-Sión was restored at the end of the 19th century, it continued to fall into disrepair. Then the citizens of Porreres decided to reactivate the monastery complex. At the start of 1954, almost the entire population of the small village took part in the building of the three-kilometre-long surfaced road high in the mountains.

Today, the monastery is mainly used for events, primarily by the local population. On important holidays, especially around Easter, processions are held from Porreres up to the virgin of Monti-Sión. In the church, a look into the sacristy with its statues, votive tablets and pilgrim inscriptions is worthwhile.

Address 07260 Porreres, +34 (0)971 647185 | Getting there Can be reached on the Ma-5020 from Llucmajor or the Ma-5040 from Campos, 3 kilometres south of Porreres | Hours Church and monastery yard can be viewed during the day; bar and restaurant with variable opening hours | Tip It is worth a visit to the tranquil village of Porreres with the 17th-century parish church of Senyora de Consolació.

80__Albufera Canal

Pure nature far from all the hotel blocks

What seems like untouched nature today, like an oasis of primitive landscape in the middle of increasingly urbanised regions, especially on a strip of coast covered evermore in the concrete of growing hotel complexes, has already undergone substantial interventions by human hands. Parc Natural s'Albufera, the largest area of marshland on the Balearics – covering 1,700 hectares and a designated nature reserve since 1988, was originally a large freshwater lake, separated from the sea by dunes, which silted up over the course of the centuries, but never completely dried out. Today, it is a major destination for serious bird enthusiasts.

Albufera, derived from the Arabic word for lagoon 'Albuhayra', became a huge swamp area, the edges of which have always been used for agriculture since the time of the Romans. The people continually struggled with deadly malaria caused by mosquitoes. As early as the 17th century, attempts were made to control the swamp by the creation of small canals.

But the major blow was struck in the middle of the 19th century by the British firm Majorca Land Company with its engineer Frederick Bateman. He wanted to use the whole area for industry and agriculture and began to lay out a 400-kilometre-long, widely branching network of canals with over 1,000 labourers, with which the water would be directed into the streams Torrent de Muro and de Sant Miquel. Bateman and his company ultimately failed, because encroaching seawater constantly made the drying out of the area, below sea level, impossible. The largest of these man-made drainage canals, the 60-metre-wide Gran de s'Albufera Canal, runs through today's nature reserve with a length of 2.5 kilometres, and finally flows into the sea behind Pont dels Anglesos, the 'bridge of the English', and the road from Port Alcúdia to Can Picafort at s'Oberta, like a wide aisle in the landscape.

Address Carretera Alcúdia–Artà, 07458 Platjes de Muro | **Getting there** On the Ma-12 from Port d'Alcúdia to Can Picafort, park just before Hotel Parc Natural on the bridge, then by foot around one kilometre right to the visitor centre; bus 353, 354 or 355 from Pollença and Alcúdia, to Parc Natural | **Hours** Parc Natural s'Albufera Apr–Sept 9am–6pm, Oct–Mar 9am–5pm, visitor centre Sa Roca daily 9am–4pm | **Tip** Just before the bridge, follow the canal to the Sa Roca visitor centre, the reception area of s'Albufera nature park, which is prettiest when visited early in the morning. There is another smaller nature reserve between Alcúdia and Pollença, the marsh region s'Albuferata de Pollença.

81__The Barbara Weil Studio

Architect Daniel Libeskind built the studio

Who knows whether the American artist Barbara Weil, who died in 2018, would ever have gained so much attention if she hadn't had the idea of working with the internationally renowned star architect Daniel Libeskind to build her studio. At the same time, the artist, who was born in Chicago in 1933 and who had lived and worked on Mallorca since the start of the 1970s, had an imposing oeuvre to show off. She drew, painted and moulded. Her many-dimensional sculptures of fibreglass and car paint, sometimes flashy and colourful, are widely recognised today and do good business.

But the name Weil actually only became well known to a wider audience and a larger professional world when she decided to build a studio with connected gallery on her old tennis court next to her house, situated directly on the sea. A meeting with Daniel Libeskind crystallised the idea, and the result became a huge triumph. In fact, it is now hard to imagine Port d'Andratx without it. It has certainly set a successful counterpoint to the uniform urbanisation and illegally built houses on the mountain slopes that surround the picturesque harbour.

Studio Weil, constructed in 2003 on the road to the exclusive residential district of La Mola, is an extremely successful symbiosis between art and architecture. The creator of the extravagant Jewish Museum in Berlin and a major architect in the redesign of Ground Zero in New York, created an internally offset, unorthodoxly structured building with plenty of space for art here, which allows the sculptures and paintings of the artist to breathe and constantly offers the viewer new changes of perspective.

The place is full of curves, slants, window slits and surprising light. Studio Weil, this total artwork of shell and content, is equipped with a large jagged-looking window, in which one of the artist's works welcomes you.

Address Carrer Valleluz 1, Camí Sant Carles, 07157 Port d'Andratx, +34 (0)669 383490, www.studioweil.com | Getting there Ma-1 from Palma to Port d'Andratx | Hours Book at studiobweil@gmail.com | Tip Barbara Weil's sons want to make Studio Weil into an art focal point in the south-west of the island, with fixed opening times. Alongside their mother's art, they will also present changing exhibitions. Regular jazz evenings are also planned (xalocmusic@gmail.com).

82 Mirador Colomer

Bizarre views into the depths

Mirador Colomer, which awaits you at kilometre four on the 20-kilometre-long, serpentine and technically demanding route from Port de Pollença to Cap de Formentor, offers the most spectacular view in the whole of Mallorca. It is high above the sea, deep below the small rocky island of the same name and above the 16th-century Talaia d'Albercutx pirate tower. The viewing platform has numerous levels with different perspectives. The rock walls fall away steeply here, with up to 300-metre drops and views down into deep ravines. The sea whips up below, the wind thunders up top. The Mallorquins also call this the 'meeting place of the winds'.

Cap de Formentor forms the tip of the peninsula with the widely visible white lighthouse at the outermost end of the huge mass of rock that projects out far into the blue sea and towers more than 200 metres above it. The beacon of the Faro de Formentor, built in 1892, which houses a small restaurant and a bar, is the strongest of all lighthouses on the Balearic Islands with a radiant power of over 60 kilometres.

The Formentor peninsula belonged to the family of the Mallorquin poet Miquel i Llobera (1854–1922) for a long time, and he spent many years of his life on the headland. After his death in 1922, the land was sold. One of the buyers was an Argentinian, who built the legendary Hotel Formentor on the edge of Platja de Formentor in 1928. Its guests always included European celebrities from politics and the film industry, including Winston Churchill and Grace Kelly. Today, the five-star hotel belongs to the Barceló group. From 1925, the Spanish-Italian road building engineer Antonio Parietti Coll (1899–1979), who was born on Mallorca, designed and built the winding road in this unreal landscape and thus opened up Formentor for new visitors. For this endeavour, a memorial was erected to him on Mirador Colomer in 1968.

Address Carrer de Formentor, 07470 Port de Pollença | Getting there From Port de Pollença on Ma-2210, Carrer de Formentor after 4 kilometres, since 2018 access to Formentor partially closed for cars in the summer months | Hours Always viewable | Tip Antonio Parietti Coll also built the spectacular winding road to Sa Calobra in 1932, which is called 'the snake', due to its numerous hairpin bends.

83__ The Sea Museum

Battling with pirates for centuries

Far out in the bay of Port de Sóller on the northern end of the historic fishing quarter Santa Caterina, high up on a rock formation, you come upon a former chapel from the 13th century, the El Oratori de Santa Caterina d'Alexandria. It was once, with its neighbouring monastery, a rescue centre for the stranded and homeless who got stuck on Mallorca. For decades this all belonged to the military and was a restricted zone, but today it is the Museu de la Mar, the only one of its kind on the island.

The museum tells much of the history of Port de Sóllers, this almost circular, natural harbour, shielded by rock formations on both sides, which has provided natural protection over the centuries and was where the people felt most safe during the eventful history of the island. There was always a wide view over the sea from the defensive tower Miranda de Santa Caterina, so that approaching ships could be identified in good time and the cannons brought into position, if, as so often was the case, the ships contained pirates readying to plunder.

This fight against the pirates is documented in the museum, where the cannons of yore are still standing today. You can find out a lot about fishing, especially whaling, which was practised for centuries. Experience the fishermen with the catch of the day, which the restaurant owners scrabble over, in the rear harbour, every day around 5pm, and see their colourful fishing nets, laid out to dry. This is the story that the museum tells of the eternal living connection with the sea. And it documents the heyday of the harbour, when a myriad of steamships carrying oranges chugged in and out of here daily, bringing the 'gold' of the fertile valleys around Sóller to France or into the capital Palma, before the railway connection was built and when the crossing of the Tramuntana mountain range was extremely difficult and time consuming.

Address Carrer Santa Caterina d'Alexandria 50, 07108 Port de Sóller, +34 (0)971 632204 | Getting there By car to the harbour and then on foot from the pier to the viewing platform | Hours Tue–Sat 10am–3pm, Sun 10am–2pm | Tip Boats sail to Cala de Sa Calobra from the harbour and to the fascinating mouth of the Torrent de Pareis. There is a wonderful view of Port de Sóller from Mirador de ses Barques (Ma-10, kilometre 45) with eponymous restaurant and outdoor terrace (+34 (0)971 630792).

84 The Tower

Watchtower over all the yachts

The towns of Portals Nous and Bendinat located south-west of Palma, which merge with one another geographically, are probably the classiest on the island. This is where people with a lot of money meet. Some in their spacious properties behind walls and thick bougainvillea hedges, but the nouveau riche have a penchant to display their wealth on the yacht and harbour strip. Anyone who thinks they are someone will dock here in Port Portals with their luxury boat or even have their permanent lodgings here. The yacht marina of Portals Nous is the most exclusive on the whole of Mallorca and is among the top five in Europe, at least in terms of the sizes and furnishings of the boats and thus their prices. And as if to emphasise this, the owners' correspondingly flashy cars are parked in front of many yachts, frequently with chauffeur, signalling the owner is onboard. Or perhaps they are shopping in the exclusive arcades or taking lunch in one of the chic bistros. And if the owners are not around, then the crew will be scrubbing and cleaning the planks and the deck.

The berths cost between €500 and €1,000 per night depending on the size of the boat. There are rarely free berths, so the waiting list is always long.

For the normal Mallorca tourist a detour to Portals Nous is worthwhile, if only for the extraordinary boats. And a drink on the promenade is of course also affordable. The harbour tower watches over all of the luxury and the roughly 700 yachts measuring up to 60-metre-long, which on average cost around two-and-a-half million euros, but can easily reach prices of 10 and more – it is worth taking a look at the notices of the boat agencies. The whole thing is not that old at all. Marina Portals, the jetties, berths, buildings and the harbour tower at the entrance, on which the ship's bell that rung in its opening still hangs, was only created in 1986.

Address 07181 Portals Nous | **Getting there** Ma-1 Palma–Andratx, exit Portals Nous | **Tip** The terrace of the superb restaurant of the nearby Hotel Bendinat is worth a visit. Grand Café Cappuccino on the left at the entrance to the harbour is the place to be. You can also view the Castell de Bendinat from the outside.

85 __ The Quarry
Swimming and sunbathing done differently

It was all more rustic and isolated a few years ago of course. The fractured beach far below the plateau of Puig de Ros was even harder to reach, and for most people this kind of access to the sea had little to do with holidaying. This has changed since large parts of the space between the coastal road Ma-6014 from S'Arenal to Cala Pi and the sea was increasingly designated as building land and correspondingly urbanised.

Today, there are large settlements all the way down to the water, some with off-the-peg houses, but all with pools, intended not so much for tourists but for Mallorquins. These are good to best locations, even though there are no beaches in the classic sense, but instead a rather rugged and steep coastline. But that is the appeal for many people.

And so it is no big surprise that insiders swear by the rocky strip of coast as one of the most attractive swimming and sunbathing areas on the island. And there is a good reason for that. Not only has nature been creating bizarre rock formations here for millions of years – humans have been involved too. Right here, stone has been broken up, pounded and sawn for decades, probably also for the building of the cathedral of Palma. Huge, over-sized rectangular cubes, which were then transported into the capital on barges. At the time, the cathedral still bordered right on the sea. Over generations, many thousands of people worked on the completion of this monumental Gothic building. The cliffs south of today's S'Arenal became the nearest quarry.

And so today, if you beat a narrow path through the bushes on both sides below the car park and in front of the chic Mhares Sea Club, you can lie luxuriously on the flat and even stone formations and blocks of Marès stone, which have quite clearly been smoothed down by human hands. It doesn't always have to be a sandy beach.

Address Carrer del Oronella, 07609 Puig de Ros (Llucmajor) | **Getting there** From the Ma-6014 coming from S'Arenal at the Maiorís golf course (kilometre 6) turn left into Puig de Ros and then drive to Mhares Sea Club | **Hours** Always accessible, public car park | **Tip** Mhares Sea Club, which belongs to the nearby Delta Hotel, is also accessible to anyone who pays admission and is located in an absolutely privileged spot.

86 The Cross of Mallorca

The island prays to the heavens

Nothing quite symbolises the closeness of Mallorquins to God as much as the numerous mountains and hills that rise up from the plains with monasteries and churches on their plateaus – sometimes positioned with engineering cunning on their peaks. The lively island between earthly and spiritual, between hotbed of vice and proximity to God. Even the trip up to these Christian symbols is mostly spectacular. This is certainly the case for the narrow road up onto the Randa mountain with its three holy sites: Santuari de Nostra Senyora de la Gràcia monastery, Ermita de Sant Honorat and the Cura monastery right at the top. You will be rewarded with a breathtaking view in all directions, no matter which way you look. The view wanders over lush landscapes all the way to the coast, over quiet towns to the Tramuntana mountain range. By the time you reach the top you are overwhelmed.

And then in the yard in front of the church of the Cura monastery another view to heaven opens up. A contemporary symbol of deep piety and a sign of local Catholicism. A very modern sculpture, far from any cultural historic significance of the past centuries: the silver cross. An avant-garde work of art made of polished stainless steel, a tree, that seems to grow out of the ground and towers into the sky with innumerable crosses. Mallorca, or – fitting to the occasion at the time – Mallorca's youth, pays homage to God.

The roughly six-metre-tall metal sculpture *Creu de les creus de Mallorca* by the Mallorquin artist Jaume Falconer and the blacksmith Antoni Sastre was created on the occasion of World Youth Day 2011 in Madrid and consecrated by Mallorquin bishop Jesús Murgui. It shows an interleaved tree with 53 crosses – based roughly on the tree of science by Ramon Llull – whose metal roots feature the names of all of Mallorca's 53 municipalities. It is the silver cross that unites the whole island.

Address Santuari Nostra Senyora de Cura, 07004 Randa, Monastery: +34 (0)971 660994 |
Getting there From Palma on the Ma-15 to Algaida, then on the Ma-5010 towards
Llucmajor | Hours Always viewable | Tip It is worth taking a look in the souvenir shop or
monastery shop just next door. Recommended: the 40 per cent proof Licor Randa, a herbal
liqueur, which the monks supposedly created in the 13th century and which is said to have
healing powers.

87 __ The Ramon Llull Cave
Rediscovery on the holy mountain

The biography of Ramon Llull, born in Palma in 1232 (died 1316), will captivate you but will also leave you baffled. He married, had children, was tutor to the king and later an administrator in the royal household. He made a good living and apparently led a contented life. Then, at the age of 40, a sudden and radical break. He withdrew into the hermitage, high on the Puig de Randa, the holy mount, below the Santuari de Nostra Senyora de Cura monastery built in 1220 by King James I of Aragón, to live as a hermit in a cave. In search of God, at one with nature, in deep contemplation.

This is where Ramon Llull apparently achieved enlightenment, with a vision of Jesus on the cross. He put his newly won spirituality into the service of philosophy, theology and writing over the following decades, he designed world views full of deep religiosity. It was Ramon Llull who wrote in Catalan and raised it from a dialect to a literary language, over 700 years ago.

The 'Cova de Ramon Llull', which was discovered at the beginning of the 20th century and made accessible to the public, was closed again after vandalism and destruction and was almost forgotten. As the cave is on private, agriculturally used land, extensive negotiations were needed before the Insular Council, Algaida town hall and the owner of the land agreed to open up this jewel again, with commemorative stone and a figure of Ramon Llull, for anyone who is interested.

In order to reach the cave, in which the philosopher and theologian lived in deep solitude over a long period from 1270 and constructed an altar in honour of Our Lady of Cura, you walk around 10 minutes on foot. The 542-metre-tall Puig de Randa, visible from afar, with its three monasteries and the cave of Ramon Llull is Mallorca's second most important pilgrimage site after Lluc monastery in the Tramuntana mountain range.

Address Santuari Nostra Senyora de Cura, 07004 Randa, Monastery: +34 (0)971 660994 | Getting there From Palma on the Ma-15 to Algaida, then on the Ma-5010 towards Llucmajor, through the town of Randa up to the monastery, signposted | Hours Cave daily 10am–2pm, key available at the reception of the guesthouse or in the café-restaurant Santuari de Cura (+34 (0)971 120260) | Tip A good restaurant with Mallorquin dishes is Es Reco de Randa at the foot of the mountain (Carrer Font 21).

88__ The Grand Piano

Concerts of a different kind in the south

A salon concert at the Finca Pescador in S'Alqueria Blanca. A small music hall connected to the main building, like a chapel, the audience curiously interested, and spotlit on the stage a shiny black Ibach 'Richard Wagner' grand piano from 1912. The programme: musical fantasies by Chopin, Debussy, Mozart and Schubert. But no pianist. The concert begins. Everything that the audience hears is set into motion by a black box positioned in front of the piano, felt-covered wooden fingers on the keyboard, metal feet on the pedals. And an intricate turning punched paper roll as storage medium, the 'piano roll'. Original music from 100 years ago played by acclaimed pianists – in the case of Debussy, by the master himself.

In 1904 the firm of Welte & Söhne from Freiburg, Germany, caused a worldwide sensation, which lasted to the end of the 1920s, before the record began its triumphant march. They had developed a process that could record and replay 'all the subtleties of a pianist's personal playing style' on paper rolls: the reproduction apparatus 'Welte-Mignon'. Using an electric-powered pneumatic system, the playback of music in almost authentic sound quality and keyboard expression was possible.

Around 5,500 pieces of music on perforated paper rolls were recorded for this technology, some by the best composers and pianists of their time.

The German music enthusiast Klaus Fischer owns around 800 of these pieces of music, including works by Maurice Ravel, Claude Debussy and Gustav Mahler, who played their own pieces – and one of the few 'Welte-Mignon-Vorsetzer' that still exists. The passionate collector of self-playing music automata, all of which can be marvelled at in the finca, makes his treasures accessible to anyone who is interested and regularly organises 'Welte-Mignon' concerts, which have developed into a real insider tip among music enthusiasts.

Address Finca Pescador, 07601 S'Alqueria Blanca | **Getting there** From Santanyí on the Ma-19 to S'Alqueria Blanca | **Hours** Viewing only by appointment or via Ingrid Flohr, Arte y Cultura, +34 (0)690 218709 and +34 (0)971 074647 | **Tip** It's worth taking a detour to the picturesque Cala Figuera with the high cliff harbour entrance. Recommended: Bar Cala, a charming bar run by the same family for decades (Virgen del Carmen 59, +34 (0)971 645018).

89__The Bicycle Promenade

All the way to Palma by the edge of the water

The bicycle path leads right along the beach promenade on the Bay of Palma, from S'Arenal via Las Maravillas to Can Pastilla, the heart of Platja de Palma, planted with palm trees and, since a while back, traffic-calmed almost all the way. From Megapark, Ballermann and Schinkenstrasse, a 6-kilometre-long, up to 40-metre-wide white sandy beach opens up, at a decent distance from the numerous hotels. You can stop at any time, push your bike into the sand and quickly jump into the water. Or take a break in one of the 15 balnearios and refresh yourself with a cooling drink. Bikes for experienced and beginner cyclists alike can be rented from one of the numerous cycling shops along Platja de Palma.

Just beyond the promenade of Can Pastilla you will come across a huge site that hasn't been built on, resembling a moon landscape. Here you can ride under the most important approach path to Palma airport. It's worth making a longer stop, as the aeroplanes float one after another, almost within your grasp right over your head, as if drawn along a string of pearls.

On it goes around the harbour of Cala Gamba, where small sailing boats are moored alongside fishing boats. Picturesque bays await you all the way, where you can go for a swim without any complications. The route continues via Ciutat Jardi and the Bay of Es Molinar to Portixol; the city beach of Palma already opens up behind the port. Now you cycle higher up along the start of the quay wall, and then Palma cathedral appears too. The perfectly upgraded bicycle path leads along Port de Palma to the other end of the city and the cruise ship port. Always on permanent concrete and granules, the track is red with a white stripe marked down the middle.

This cycling tour could of course be the springboard for a swimming excursion in the Bay of Palma and perhaps a ride to S'Arenal.

Address S'Arenal–Platja de Palma–Palma and back | **Getting there** Bus 15, 17, 23 or 31 from Palma to Platja de Palma and back | **Hours** Best to cycle in daylight, as most rental bikes don't have lights | **Tip** Call into one of the small restaurants in the port of the picturesque village of Es Molinar for a salad. A little more sophisticated: Puro Beach Club, located on a headland on the outermost end of Can Pastilla. Elegant, white loungers, swimming in pool and sea, quality cuisine.

90 Porciúncula

Modern architecture on the Schinkenstrasse

There is hardly anything of much interest to see on the almost six-kilometre-long Platja de Palma, the east coast strip of Palma between Can Pastilla and S'Arenal with its 15 so-called Balnearios, apart from hotels, pubs, shops, sand and beach. And yet, hidden a little off the beaten track in this corner of the island is an unusual church, that you should take a look at. A church not like the small and large cathedrals in Palma, old, sublime, full of cultural historic treasures and lots of buried celebrities from the gruesome past. No, a modern church. Something like this exists, amazingly, in the neighbourhood of Beach Club Six and Schinkenstrasse.

The Catholic Porciúncula, part of the Franciscan Order, is also commonly referred to as the 'glass church', which is dedicated to 'Our Lady of the Angels'. The church, created in 1968, was originally conceived as a seminary for preparing students for the priesthood. Built of concrete and 600 square metres of glass, mainly stained glass, it is architecturally modern and thus daring for a sacred Mallorquin building. The rotunda, whose altar stands in the middle, is surrounded by 39 large, stained-glass windows that reach all the way up to the vaulted ceiling, which represent numerous motifs relating to Saint Francis and to the creation story. The floor is decorated with marble tiles that show fish motifs.

The glass church is part of the adjacent La Porciúncula park, a shady oasis of calm and recuperation from the stresses of beach life. The park was laid out in 1914 by the Franciscans when they were building a branch of their monastery in Palma.

Today, the Porciúncula complex includes a small museum with archaeological pottery and finds from the missionary work of the Franciscans in South America. The Porciúncula monastery additionally contains an educational centre with theology college, a kindergarten and a school.

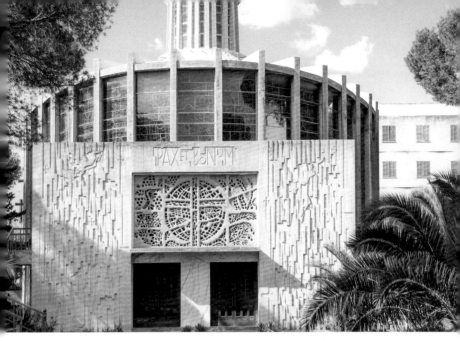

Address La Porciúncula, Avinguda Fray Joan Llabrés 1, 07600 S'Arenal, +34 (0)971 260002 | Getting there Bus 15 from Plaça de la Reina, bus 26 from Plaça d'Espanya, to Porciúncula; by car, pull off in Las Maravillas (motorway exit 11) | Hours June–Aug Mon–Sat 9.30am–1pm & 3.30–6.45pm; Sept–May Mon–Sat 3.30–6pm, Sun 9.30am–1pm | Tip From Arenal it is worth taking a trip to the ostrich farm Artestruz, which is on Carretera Cabo Blanco, kilometre 40, near Campos.

91 The Sleeping Madonna
Emerging from meditation after an eternity

In Sant Crist church in the quaint hamlet of S'Arracó not far from Andratx on the way to Sant Elm, something wondrous occurred a few years ago, which moved the Catholic congregation to delight and appreciation. The serving priest and some of the older members of the congregation recalled that in the mid-1960s, the church's reclining Madonna was packed up without further ado in a crate and stowed in the loft of the church in order to save her from falling into disrepair. It turned out that the Sant Crist church in S'Arracó owns one of the very rare examples of a 'Mare de Déu Morta', which can only be found in a few churches on Mallorca, such as in the cathedrals in Palma and the churches of Santanyí and Valdemossa.

The veneration connected with the 'sleeping Madonna' is probably unique to Mallorca. The Madonnas, which usually lie in a side altar, are laid in state on 15 August around Assumption Day for one week in the main nave of the church. This is now also happening again with the Madonna from S'Arracó, which is considered especially valuable in terms of art history, and dates from the year 1528. The then renowned Spanish sculptor and Renaissance artist Joan de Salas had made 'Dormitio Mariae' for the Santa María de la Real monastery in Palma. The Madonna first came to S'Arracó in 1835 in the course of secularisation and the closing of Palma's large monasteries, when a monk brought it here to protect it from being taken and destroyed.

The priest from S'Arracó has now decided to show the 'sleeping Madonna' to the faithful not only for Assumption Day, and to make it accessible to all who are interested. For S'Arracó this means a real gem that is worth visiting. So now the Madonna lies in a side altar of Sant Crist church, clearly visible inside a glass case, with her blue cloak and golden halo, barefoot and hands folded.

Address Plaça General Weyler, 07159 S'Arracó | Getting there On the Ma-1030 from Andratx to Sant Elm; bus IB 35 from Andratx | Hours Irregular opening hours, church services always Sundays at 10am | Tip The large Art Nouveau houses near the church are impressive. It's worth taking a trip to Sant Elm. From here you can get the ferry to Sa Dragonera island.

92__ The Devil Masks
Mixing pagan and religious traditions

For some time now the Museu Sant Antoni has been part of the new cultural centre of Can Planes in the middle of Sa Pobla. There is generally not much going on in Sant Antoni, and so the lights in the darkened room often have to be turned on when you arrive, before you can tentatively immerse yourself in the world of gigantic devils and fantasy figures, which await you, snarling, sneering and ready to attack. It leaves behind a real impression. As does watching the short, remarkable film, which explains, powerfully accentuated by the music, what these devils and fanciful figures are all about, if they were to be set free and revived. Like every year in the night from 16 to 17 January. This is when, in the otherwise rather sleepy Sa Pobla, all hell breaks loose, in the fullest sense of the word.

This is the night of Sant Antoni – an excessive and elaborate fiesta into the early hours of the morning, which is celebrated here like nowhere else. Demons run through the narrow alleyways, red devils, dancing ecstatically and high-spiritedly. Huge masks, figures with over-sized heads, the 'Caparrots', traditional folk characters and the mythological monster 'el Grifo'. And Saint Anthony as the main character, and devils, over and over. Fire everywhere, huge pyres smoulder, gigantic fireworks explode, flames flicker. Then there's the music of the ximbombades, instruments made of a clay pot covered with a rabbit or goat skin, and rhythmic Mallorquin chants.

That night, Saint Anthony fights against the evil powers and temptation, banishes the demons and the winter, becoming the victor of light over darkness. He's been doing it since 1375. Saint Anthony is also the patron saint of animals, which are blessed during this night, a special feast day for agriculture. Then the devil costumes and large-headed dolls disappear again for a year into the Sant Antoni museum.

Address Can Planes, Carrer Antoni Maura 6, 07420 Sa Pobla, +34 (0)971 542389 | Getting there Bus or train Palma–Inca-Sa Pobla; buses from Muro and Port d'Alcúdia; by car on the Ma-13 | Hours Tue–Fri 10am–2pm & 4–8pm, Sat & Sun 10am–2pm | Tip The Can Planes culture centre also contains a museum of contemporary art, a toy museum and studios for courses and seminars.

93 The Black Pigs

Meet them at the Els Calderers country estate

In contrast to the neighbouring cities of Petra and Sineu for example, which await with important cultural treasures, Sant Joan is all about the sausage. Agriculture is dominant here: this is the home of the famous blood sausage 'Botifarrónes' and the 'Sobrasada de Mallorca', a sausage speciality that you can only get on Mallorca, whose geographic origin is protected by the European Union and can only be produced here. It is famous far beyond the island and an attractive souvenir for tourists.

The Sobrasada is sausage made from the black pig, 'porc negre', a special breed that traditionally only exists on Mallorca in this variety. And the sausage has to be made according to a very particular recipe with a strict list of ingredients. Sant Joan and its surroundings are the stronghold of pig breeding and the sausage factories, of which there are around a dozen.

And those who would like to meet a black pig should head towards the country estate of Els Calderers, located just beyond Sant Joan and below the Puig de Bonany hermitage, which can be traced back to the 13th century. The feudal manor house, which has been open to the public since the mid-1990s, was built in 1750 and belonged to the aristocratic Verí family, who expanded it ever further for generations. Alongside the impressive, elaborately furnished manor house, which gives you the feeling of travelling 200 years back in time over several floors, Els Calderers includes numerous out buildings, a large Mallorquin kitchen for the staff, the granary, different workshops with old machines, a chapel, and a wine cellar. Everything gives you the impression that the estate was only left yesterday, as if its occupants could come back at any moment. But the only places with any real life left in them are the numerous stables. This is where, among others, the famous black pigs are bred. Why not come and say hello?

Address Els Calderers, 07240 Sant Joan, +34 (0)971 526069 | Getting there Ma-15 Carretera Palma–Manacor, exit and signpost at kilometre 37 | Hours Apr–Oct 10am–6pm, Nov–Mar 10am–5pm | Tip Just before Sant Joan is the small Santuari de la Mare Déu de Consolació church, built in the 13th century and recently renovated.

94__ The Jewish Cemetery

The Jews of Mallorca went through hard times

In the year 1978, Mallorca's Jewish community, which comprises around 200 families today, managed to acquire an acre of land and created their cemetery in Santa Eugènia, traditionally a centre for Jews on the island. Just behind the village's communal parish cemetery, this, the only Jewish cemetery, lies peacefully behind a wrought iron gate with Hebrew characters on it.

There had been a large Jewish community on Mallorca for centuries, but after the Reconquista from the middle of the 12th century, they were increasingly subjected to persecution. Four synagogues in Palma represented Jewish life in the Middle Ages, which played a large role in money lending and in the gold and silver trade – with the consequence that many Christians were in large debt to Jews. From 1300, tensions escalated, and although the Jews were tolerated by the king and vested with privileges, pogroms began to occur quite frequently. At the start of the 15th century the Jewish community was made up of over 1,000 families.

In 1435 catastrophe struck. Hundreds of Jews were murdered, many were forced to convert to Christianity, but the 'secret Jews', the 'Xuetes' survived. With the Inquisition there were virtually no more Jews left on Mallorca, but the Xuetes were also continuously subjected to persecution.

Many German Jews emigrated to Mallorca from 1933 in the hope of safe refuge. But the Nazis who had lived here since the Spanish Civil War, former members of the Condor Legion, worked actively as spies for Germany. In mid-1940, Hitler demanded that Spanish General Franco make Mallorca 'Jew-free' and deport all Jews. For most this meant certain death. The German demand even included Jews whose families were forced into conversion in the Middle Ages, but the Spanish defied this. There has been a small Jewish community on Mallorca again since 1971, the first since 1435.

ברוך

ישראל על יקיצ

ריוט שוכבי עפר

Address Camí de Cementeri, 07142 Santa Eugènia, Jewish community: Comunidad Judaía de Mallorca, Carrer de Monsenyor Palmer 3, 07014 Palma, +34 (0)629 694058 | Getting there From Palma on the Ma-3011 towards Sineu, exit on the Ma-3040 | Hours The cemetery is usually closed, but you can take a look through the wrought iron gate | Tip A short walk through Santa Eugènia with its two outstanding windmills is worthwhile.

95 __ The Wine Express

A road train through wine growing country

The Romans brought wine growing to Mallorca, and in the Middle Ages the wine trade experienced such a boom that the majority of rural jobs were in wine production. In the 19th century, Mallorquin wine, especially the sweet Malvasía grapes, ultimately became a real success. Dessert wines from Mallorca were also a hit on the Spanish mainland. Then, around 1900, phylloxera hit the island and destroyed almost all of the Mallorquin wine in production, from the vine fields of Pla and the vine terraces of the plateau to the Tramuntana mountain range. Wine growing on Mallorca was practically wiped out. It took a long time until the island was able to recover.

However, since the 1980s, wine growing has been vigorously and extensively rehabilitated, the vineyards recultivated and the old bodegas resurrected. The intention was to pick up the threads of the centuries-old tradition of Mallorquin viniculture. Today, Mallorquin wines are once again well established, and those from the area surrounding Binissalem are of particular quality. You will find two of the island's largest bodegas in this region, with the Ferrer and Macià Batle vineyards, both privately run. There are also many smaller wine estates that produce both white and red wine of equally high quality. That is almost guaranteed by the Mediterranean climate.

You can now explore the vineyards of the Binissalem region twice a day on the trackless road train. So all aboard the 'Mallorca Wine Express': you drive through the fields and vineyards, find out interesting facts about wine and viniculture, watch the vintners at work and of course taste fine wines and, if desired, buy them too. The road train chugs along its route for two hours, starting in the yard in front of the Macià Batle estate, and calling at various bodegas, including addresses such as Can Rubi, Vins Nadal and Ribas.

Address Camí de Coanegra, 07320 Santa Maria del Camí, +34 (0)653 528659 (www.mallorcawinetours.com) or +34 (0)971 140014 (Macià Batle estate) | **Getting there** Ma-13 from Palma to Alcúdia, exit Santa Maria del Camí; train from Palma to Inca or from Manacor via Inca to Palma | **Hours** Please call for tour times | **Tip** It is definitely worth taking a guided tour of Macià Batle bodega, one of the biggest on Mallorca, with wine tasting and food (+34 (0)971 140014).

96 The Stone Cross

King James I landed here and beat the Arabs

Beyond all the tourist hustle and bustle and the seemingly uncontrollable building boom around the rocky Bay of Santa Ponça, with its sandy beach, is a memorial that gives a deep insight into the history of the island.

A part of the medieval history of Mallorca, which continues to have a significant effect to this day, began right here, where the large white cross stands resplendent and visible from afar. In the Bay of Santa Ponça, right next to the chic yacht harbour and Club Nàutic, is where the troops of James I of Aragón landed on 12 September, 1229, in order to recapture the island for Christianity and to expel the Muslim Moors who had ruled for three centuries. Here, at the end of the small Sa Caleta peninsula is where the Reconquista, the bloody battle for Mallorca, began. The Arab troops were beaten and Palma was eventually captured.

The white stone cross, Cruz de la Conquista, was dedicated in 1929 on the 700th anniversary of the landing of the king, his 150 ships and the military force of 15,000 men. This is where the first flag of the king was apparently hoisted on the island. Various events from during the recapture of Mallorca are represented, as well as the celebration of the first Holy Mass on Mallorquin ground, on the eight stone reliefs on the pedestal of the cross. A large stone block is still preserved as a relic in the Capilla de la Piedra Sagrada, the 'chapel of the holy stone', in the centre of the city, on which, according to lore, the first mass after the landing of the king and his troops was held.

Ever since, the invasion of 1229 is evoked in the Moros i Cristians celebrations every first weekend in September. The landing of the Christian ships and the first battles between Moors and Christians and the successful re-Christianisation is reenacted on the beach, complemented by the large Rei de Jaume festival.

Address Via de la Creu, 07180 Santa Ponça | Getting there On the Ma-1 from Palma to Andratx, exit Ma-1013 to Santa Ponça, then on Via de la Creu to Sa Caleta to the yacht marina | Tip Those who find the beach of Santa Ponça too full should try the beaches of Portals Vells, which are above the Caps de Cala Figuera.

97 — The Jordi Bosch Organ

Heavenly sounds in the Sant Andreu church

The organ of Sant Andreu church in Santanyí is considered the finest on the island. Its sound is hailed as heavenly, it is otherworldly, people claim rapturously. It is praised by organists who have played on it, organ builders who have tried to achieve similar results, and listeners who have been lucky enough to attend many concerts on different organs in equal measure. But the organ of Sant Andreu, this 18th-century church on Plaça Major in Santanyí, is very much of this world, and is in fact a masterpiece by the highly talented and musically adept Mallorquin organ builder Jordi Bosch (1736–1800), who achieved fame and recognition far beyond the shores of Mallorca from early on, which ultimately saw him advance to royal organ builder. The Santanyí organ, which dates from 1762, was his first very large work, which immediately marked him out as exceptional in this highly complex profession. Jordi Bosch, who came from an organ building family and later built the organs of the cathedrals of Seville and the organ in the royal palace of Madrid, was only 26 years old at the time.

Bosch had actually built the organ for the Santo Domingo monastery in Palma, but after the closure of the Dominican monastery in 1837, it was sold to and stored in Santanyí. It wasn't until 50 years later that the organ was reactivated again, initially in slimmed-down form with a few keyboards. But the complicated instrument was treated unprofessionally and required a thorough refurbishment. In 1984, the organ was finally restored by the renowned German organ builder Gerhard Grenzing and returned to its full glory. Today, the organ presents itself as a visual showpiece, but primarily it captivates listeners with its unique tone quality, which fills the church to its furthest corners. Its unique trumpets in particular create the bright triumphant sound that Jordi Bosch devised 250 years ago.

Address Plaça Major 31, 07650 Santanyí, +34 (0)971 653152 | Getting there Ma-19 motorway Palma–Llucmajor, then the Carretera via Campos to Santanyí | Hours The church opens irregularly during the day. There are many organ concerts in Sant Andreu | Tip The predecessor church from the 14th century, Capella de Roser, which is adjacent and connected to Sant Andreu church, is worth seeing.

98_ The Stone Horses
The unusual sculpture of Rolf Schaffner

There's a treasure lying dormant in Santanyí. It's not so easy to find, but once you've discovered it, you'll struggle to get over your amazement. If you drive on the road to Es Llombards in a southerly direction and pass the roundabout with the *Rey y Reina* sculptures, you will find an area on the left that looks quite wild and overgrown. If you strike a path through the bushes for a few metres, they suddenly appear before you: the *Caballos*, seven huge horses made of natural layered stone. And this proud herd has stood here since 1963. That's when the German artist and sculptor Rolf Schaffner (1927–2008), who lived and worked in Santanyí for over four decades, created this unusual sculpture, which has become so overgrown in the meantime.

You can find another 'impossible' sculpture garden on the left-hand side of the road from Santanyí to Campos, after around three kilometres, just before the hamlet of Son Danusset. At first sight, it feels as though you have been transported into a prehistoric epoch or catapulted into the Aztec culture of Central America. Monumental stone blocks, piled one on top of the other to form objects up to six metres tall stand among almond and olive trees, and wild growing bushes. This is 'Son Danús', the open plot that was studio and exhibition space in one for Rolf Schaffner. (Viewings via Gallery Flohr in Santanyí, +34 (0)690 218709.)

The German-born sculptor's main material was this yellowy-red stone, inspired by the diverse stone structures on the island and by the drystone walling that has often been used through all the historic epochs on the island. His ingenious stone layering and creation of various forms cannot be clearly classified, oscillating between land art and abstract sculpture, between archaic and contemporary. *Rey y Reina* on the roundabout near Santanyí towards Es Llombards is also by Schaffner.

Address 07650 Santanyí | Getting there Road from Santanyí to Campos, kilometre 47 (sculpture park) | Tip The oversized sculpture on Cala Santanyí, not far from the Es Pontas rocks, is one of Schaffner's last pieces and forms the most southerly point of his international sculpture project *Equilibrio* (*Meridians of Peace*) in five places in Europe.

99__The Shoe Museum
The slow decline of a proud craft

The shoe and leather factory Kollflex, or what is left of it, still belongs to the founding Coll family. So you may still meet some grandchild or relative of the shoemaking dynasty today in the large outlet store of the former manufacturer on the road to Lluc at the end of Selva. But in reality, nothing is like it was, back when the Kollflex shoe factory, which Lorenzo Coll founded in 1927 in a small workshop at the foot of the Tramuntana mountain range, was booming and the shoes from Selva could hold their own with the big brands from Inca and were in demand throughout the country and even Europe. Shoe production was in the DNA of the region for over a hundred years.

While some of the larger brands like Camper or Lottuse still sell well – although they are not produced on Mallorca any more, rather predominantly in low-wage countries – the small, privately owned factories are finding things difficult. Not least because of the competition from Asia. Ten years ago there were still 130 employees working at Kollflex – a thousand pairs of shoes were still being produced by hand every day in Selva. Today, it is only four. The large factory hall was closed in 2010. Now external manufacturers produce around 1,500 pairs – a year – for the outlet store.

Part of the old Kollflex production hall – for many decades the biggest employer in the municipality of Selva, with the wonderful 14th-century Sant Llorenc parish church – was repurposed as a small museum by the Coll grandchildren. On display are old machines, exhibits of production and parts of past shoe collections. At the centre of the permanent exhibition: the sculpture *Mans, Mans, Mans, Peus*, which reaches all the way to the roof, by the artist Joan Lacomba from Selva. The tower of shoes is his homage to the many thousands of men and women who have dedicated their lives to the production of handmade shoes.

Address Museo del Calzado, Carretera de Lluc 47, 07313 Selva, +34 (0)971 515734,
www.kollflex1927.com | Getting there From Palma the Ma-13 to Inca, then the Ma-2130
to Selva, through the village towards Lluc, on the left at the end of town | Hours Summer:
Mon–Sat 9am–8pm, Sun 9am–2pm; winter: Mon–Fri 9.30am–7pm, Sun 9.30am–2pm,
admission free, guided tours for groups of 15 or more people | Tip In 2010, the shoe and
leather museum in Inca opened with a permanent exhibition in Cuartel General Luque,
an old military barracks from 1915 (Museu del Calçat, Carrer Luque 225, Mon–Fri
10am–2pm & 4–8pm, Sat 10am–1pm, admission free). The Monumento al los Zapateros
standing on Plaza Sa Quartera in Inca is in honour of the shoemakers and their craft.

100__ The Brewery

Belgian beer from the heart of Mallorca

Small breweries are springing up like mushrooms all over Mallorca and seem to find a willing and thirsty clientele. It doesn't always have to be the established brands of Estrella, San Miguel or Mahou. There are around ten of these microbreweries on the island, producing their hand-brewed beers, which are called 'Cerveza Artesana' in Spanish. Craft beer is now in great demand on Mallorca.

But the only place to find homemade Belgian beer is in Cas Canar, a tiny hamlet near Sencelles. The Belgian Michel Campioni and three employees have been brewing six different beers here since 2017.

Brewing was always a passion of the architect from the Belgian town of Eupen, who organised the international shop fitting for the Mallorquin shoe and leather producers Camper for many years and thus always had a connection to the island. Campioni, who settled on Mallorca 20 years ago, always had the secret goal of making his hobby of brewing beer into a profession. He bought a vacant bodega in Cas Canar, pepped it up and tilled the land around it. Then he came upon the idea of converting the old building into a brewery. With great success.

After a long trial period, the Belgian now produces six different craft beers in his small but highly modern brewery. Alongside the usual malt and hops, the beer also contains flavours and ingredients from his own Mallorquin farm. A distributor places the beers in numerous food and drink markets around the island. Of course, all of the beers are also available in the Toutatis taproom, which is in a perfect location. There is nothing on offer to eat except peanuts, but there is a large barbecue garden with grill areas and paella pans. And it's real hit: at weekends the Mallorquins come in their droves, bringing their own food with them to barbecue and cook. The only condition: the beer has to be bought from Michel.

Address Toutatis, 07140 Sencelles/Cas Canar, +34 (0)649 412338 | Getting there From Palma on the Ma-13 towards Inca, Sencelles exit, at the end of Sencelles on the Ma-3140 and 3 kilometres further to Cas Canar, large car park | Hours Wed–Fri 5–11pm, Sat noon–11pm, Sun noon–10pm, beer tasting and brewery tours all year round, booking essential | Tip Alfonso Munoz Murillo has brewed three different craft beers in nearby Sineu (Placa des Fossar 20) since the end of 2018; in María de la Salut (Travessia d'Antonio Monjo) the German Ralf Breede brews two beers. Mallorca's observatory is in Costix, the central point of the island.

101 __ The Es Trenc Bunker

History draws you in on an idyllic beach

The roughly five-kilometre-long beach Es Trenc, between Ses Covetes and Colònia de Sant Jordi, is considered by many Mallorca experts as the island's most fascinating stretch of coastline. It is the longest undeveloped beach on Mallorca. Its fans swear by the fine white sand, the bordering dune landscape with its bizarre beach grass vegetation and the many pine forests. A conservation area that extends from the beach to a few kilometres inland protects it from property speculation and the building boom. In contrast, Ses Covetes, the place you are most likely to call in at from Es Trenc, was once scattered with numerous illegally built summer houses. Their construction was stopped at some point and they are now all being torn down. Building ruins right by the sea next to restaurants, beach shacks and some legal dwellings. That was just too much in the end.

Surprisingly, you will encounter very different ruins during a walk on the beach, between the edge of the water and where the sand dunes accumulate. Large old bunkers, cubes of poured concrete, with thick walls, seemingly impregnable. Two narrow vertical crenellations mark the place from which machine guns protruded, ready to engage with approaching enemy ships or landing soldiers. Some tourists seek protection from the sun in the shade of the concrete, others lie naked nearby, as parts of the beach are designated nudist areas. But not many people know the story of these bunkers, when and why these bizarre giants were erected on this protected beach reserve. The bunkers were built between 1940 and 1950. The reason: the fascist Franco dictatorship always feared that the victorious Allies, who had defeated fascism in Germany and Italy, would have Spain next on their list, not least because of their role in the Spanish Civil War (1936–1939), when the Francoists overthrew the Republic in a bloody rebellion.

Address Platja Es Trenc, 07639 Ses Covetes or 07638 Colònia de Sant Jordi | Getting there Take the access road to Es Trenc beach from the Campos to Colònia Sant Jordi road or from Campos towards Sa Ràpita via the Ses Covetes access road | Tip On the way to Colonia de Sant Jordi, beyond the salt pans, is another path to Es Trenc with a large car park in front of the dunes. East of Ses Covetes you will find Platja de Sa Ràpita, a beach with a similar structure as Es Trenc, which is also a nature reserve.

102 The Cactus Farm

You can get them in all sizes at Toni Moreno's

Looking out over the wide open cactus fields behind the inviting finca and the large greenhouses, you may feel a bit like you're in Arizona or New Mexico. Like in the setting of a Warner Brothers spaghetti western. But certainly not like you're on Mallorca, the island of sun, with its lush landscape, which is generally characterised by palms, olives and almond trees, by citrus fruits and vineyards, by fertile valleys and fast-flowing streams. You won't find anything like Toni Moreno's finca on the edge of Ses Salines twice on Mallorca. Cacti as far as the eye can see.

The best way to experience Toni Moreno and his unique cactus world is in the branch of the business and market garden at the end of Carrer Einstein in the village itself. There are huge greenhouses and open areas with thousands of prickly plants here too. You can buy cacti and on request receive an introduction to the fascinating lives of these plants.

Around 500 types of cactus, from giant specimens that look like statues to those for your window sill at home, grow on 40,000 square metres at the Morenos' finca. When Toni Moreno began cultivating cacti in 1972, he focused on the smaller varieties. But when daughter Antonia got onboard with her father's business, after studying in California and discovering the huge diversity of this species, there was no going back. From that point on the family cultivated the very big cacti too. Today, the Morenos have an international clientele, are one of the biggest Spanish cactus farms and deliver to countries as far off as China. Orders are carried out online and the goods are transported in shipping containers. The small family business with its four employees sells between 20,000 and 25,000 cacti a year. The larger specimens can be pretty expensive, but this should come as no surprise, considering that cacti grow very slowly and require a lot of care.

Address Cactus Toni Moreno, Carrer Einstein, 07640 Ses Salines, +34 (0)971 649280 | Getting there From Campos on the Ma-6040/Ma-6101 or from Santanyí on the Ma-6100 to Ses Salines. Coming from Campos, turn off the Ma-6100 onto Carrer Einstein at the start of town and drive through to the end of the road. | Hours Sept–Feb Mon–Fri 8.30am–12.30pm & 3–5pm, Sat 9am–noon; Mar–Sept Mon–Fri 8am–1pm, Sat 9am–noon | Tip The Botanicactus botanical gardens, which has a huge cactus garden as well as many other plants, is very near Ses Salines on the Ma-6100.

103__ The Winged Lion

A market under constant observation

The Wednesday market in Sineu is considered the best market on Mallorca – and looks back on a centuries-old tradition. This is of course due to the quality and the variety of the produce that is on offer here. After all, the little town of Sineu, which is located on a hill and forms the central geographical point of the island, is the agricultural centre of the fertile Es Pla plains. Fruit and vegetables, olives in every possible variation and combination, spices, fish and meat are all on offer on the central Plaça d'Espanya, but also in the numerous side alleys, on the steps and terraces of the picturesque medieval city.

And most of it at affordable prices. Mallorquins shop here. Of interest to tourists are the numerous stalls with handicrafts, fabrics, leather goods and ceramics. But agricultural equipment is also sold, and you can find knife grinders and potters.

The Sineu livestock market on Plaça del Fossar, the only one of its kind on Mallorca, is particularly interesting. Here goats, sheep, pigs, chickens and ducks, but also cows and horses are sold. Trade is done in a very traditional and loud manner and deals are sealed with a handshake. The farmers convey their purchases on livestock trucks, others leave the market with chickens and ducks tucked under their arms. After a successful transaction, many go straight to one of the surrounding bars and cellars, which are always packed on market day.

And placed high above all the activity of the market is the lion of Sineu. Self-assured, triumphant, and confident of victory, the bronze Lleó de Sant Marc stands here in honour of Mark the Evangelist, the patron saint of the city. The winged lion has stood guard over market and people in front of the city's most important church, the Nostra Senyora dels Àngels from the 13th century, with its huge free-standing 16th-century bell tower, since 1945.

Address Sa Plaça, 07510 Sineu | **Getting there** On the Ma-3011 from Palma or on the Ma-3320/Ma-3300 from Manacor via Petra | **Hours** Market every Wednesday morning | **Tip** You simply must see the Nostra Senyora dels Àngels church and its delightful chapels from the inside. It is also worth attending the candle spectacle 'Contrallum', which has been taking place in Sineu every November for the past four years: an open-house event where local artists exhibit extravagant art.

104 The Botanical Gardens

And a little natural history museum too

The botanical gardens in Sóller, built in 1985 and opened to the public in 1992 is a little neglected by a general public that is surrounded by the most beautiful flora on the island anyway. In the midst of mass tourism, land speculation and an evermore unrestrained, throw-away society, it's easy to lose sight of the details that are worth protecting. Intact nature is not just a matter of course on the Balearic Islands. The Botanical Gardens Sóller foundation has made it its mission to continue to research and preserve the flora of the Balearics. Worth a visit for this reason alone, it is enjoyable and instructive, and much more than just another chance to delight in nature. The Sóller botanical gardens are the only one of its kind on the Balearic Islands and an oasis of peace away from all the commotion of tourism.

What you will see are almost all plants that grow wild on the Balearics, including species threatened by extinction. The fauna of the rocky and coastal regions of the island is exciting. The Sóller botanical gardens are characterised by four important collections: the collection of living plants, all the important medicinal plants in the ethnobotanical area, culinary plants and ornamental plants. In a germplasm bank, the seeds of endangered plant species are preserved as well as a genetic reserve of traditional fruit, vegetable and grain varieties – as a guarantee of biological diversity on the islands. Then there is the herbarium and the iconographic and bibliographic collection. The Sóller botanical gardens also has an important collection of the plants of the Canary Islands.

The modern natural science museum in the former manor house on the grounds of the botanical gardens presents an outstanding collection of fossils and holds a reference library for scientists. Here, introductions to botany are also regularly taught to school classes.

Address Fundació Jardí Botànic de Sóller, Carretera Palma–Port de Sóller, 07100 Sóller, +34 (0)971 634014 | Getting there From Palma on the Ma-11 or Ma-10 to Sóller; train from Station Placa Espanya; bus L 210 or L 211 | Hours Mar–Oct Mon–Sat 10am–6pm, Nov–Feb Tue–Sat 10am–2pm, guided tours possible | Tip A trip on the Sóller–Port de Sóller tram, which has been rolling along the tracks since 1913 and departs every half an hour in summer and every 60 minutes in winter, is fun. Fet a Sóller, producer and distributor of delicatessen and specialities of Mallorquin origin, has three shops in Sóller, Port d'Sóller and Palma (+34 (0)971 638839, www.fetasoller.com).

105 Can Prunera

Competition for Es Baluard in Tramuntana

Everything fits together in these narrow streets in the centre of Sóller: the interior of this fine museum of modern art and the Art Nouveau villa built in 1911 by a local businessman. Created in a period when the wealthy of the city, who had made their fortunes abroad, returned home and began to compete for who owned the most beautiful house in Sóller. This magnificent villa with its impressive façade and the artfully painted reliefs stands so tall in this narrow road that you have to crane your neck in order to take in the whole thing. And the house is in a class of its own. Consistently the most beautiful Art Nouveau design, right down to the smallest detail, and all original. The colourful, ornamented glass windows, the tiled floor, the curved staircase, the meticulously restored furniture. And since 2009 it has also housed one of the most wonderful museums on the island.

Through the different rooms of Can Prunera are displays of Art Nouveau objects by local and international artists, Catalan modernism, Joan Miró's book illustrations, a significant collection of antique dolls and high-quality exhibits of modern art. Picasso, Miró, Magritte, Léger, Barceló, Nolde, as well as selected works by Jordi Rames, one of the most important Mallorquin artists of the first half of the 20th century. The delightfully laid out garden contains a dozen unconventional sculptures. Around two-thirds of these pictures and objects are from the Serra collection and were originally on show in Es Baluard museum in Palma, whose mentor was Pedro Serra. But then the major patron of the arts and influential publisher of the Serra media group, which also publishes the *Mallorca Magazine*, fell out with Palma's art management team and withdrew parts of his loan. Since then these pieces have been on show in Can Prunera, which he co-founded and which is owned by Fundació Tren de l'Art.

Address Carrer de Sa Lluna 86 and 90, 07100 Sóller, +34 (0)971 638973, www.canprunera.com | **Getting there** Coming from the railway station (Estació del Tren de Sóller) over Plaça d'Espanya and Plaça Sa Constitució into Carrer de la Lluna | **Hours** Daily 10.30am–6pm | **Tip** It is definitely worth visiting the centre of Sóller with more examples of the finest Art Nouveau architecture, especially Sant Bartolomé church. From here, why not take a trip to the picturesque village of Fornalutx.

106__ The Dune Beach
Peace far from the big hotel complexes

If there weren't any mountains in the background, you might be forgiven for thinking you are on an island in northern Germany or Denmark. Wonderful sandy beaches and picturesque bays are in ample supply on Mallorca, but a dune landscape like the one at Son Serra de Marina is rather more rare. And what is more, the nature reserve of the one-and-a-half-kilometre-long beach with dune landscape stretching far inland and the occasional pine forest, which begins on the eastern edge of the town just beyond the Torrent de na Borges, is not overcrowded, and nigh on deserted in the off-season. You can walk to the obelisks that stand far back in the dunes and feel like you aren't really on Mallorca. You won't come across any beach bars or snack stands, which is what makes it so appealing, so you should take your own picnic basket with you. You're bound to enjoy a day out of a very different nature.

The only really appealing aspect of the small town Son Serra de Marina, an outright holiday resort, architecturally designed on the drawing board and set into the landscape, is that all of the houses are roughly the same height, so there are no large hotel complexes. All the roads in town lead directly to the sea. They are predominantly private houses, holiday homes. A town of around 1,000 inhabitants in summer, but in the off season it is almost empty. Then you'd be lucky to even see another person, as Son Serra de Marina is like a ghost town. A few inhabitants spend the winter here, others check that everything's all right at the weekend.

But Son Serra de Marina is never really uncomfortably overrun in summer either. There are no overcrowded beaches, so it is quite the contrast to nearby Can Picafort. The infrastructure is correspondingly sparse, with just a supermarket, a pharmacy, a bakery and a limited range of eating out options, as well as a small sport and yacht harbour.

Address Platja de sa Canova, 07450 Son Serra de Marina | Getting there Ma-12 Alcúdia via Can Picafort to Artà, exit Son Serra de Marina; buses from Can Picafort. You can park right on the edge of the beach at the eastern end of town. | Tip Platja de Son Real is another dune beach, which can only be reached on foot, to the west towards Son Bauló. At the start of Platja de sa Canova is the sunshine bar El Sol, a Caribbean-inspired beach bar with restaurant, which is also open in winter.

107 __ Església Nova
The unfinished church – now an open-air stage

A church without a roof and with open windows, though highly regarded architecturally, with a massive bold curved frontage, in the middle of the city and yet almost impossible to understand from the road. Església Nova, the new, unfinished church in Son Servera, this small charming town not far from the coast in the east of the island, which was fought for so bloodily in the Spanish Civil War.

In 1905, the Catalan architect Joan Rubió i Bellver (1870–1952) was given the contract to construct another house of God alongside the parish church Sant Joan Bautista, which had been there since the 18th century. The architect, who was a close colleague of Antoni Gaudí (1852–1926), began to construct a church in the neo-Gothic style.

What you can see today is a church nave in strict simplicity, with huge church windows, pointed arches and rosettes, but all open to the heavens. And what might be the reason for this? Simply, that the developers ran out of money. Construction carried on until 1929, when it was abandoned for good. So the church stands there today, for some a ruin, for others a modern, almost *avant-garde* structure. People in Son Servera have become used to its state, and all the flickering initiatives that pop up every now and then to maybe complete the church after all are regularly rejected. It would lose its uniqueness, lose its fascination, become one church among many others if it were no longer open to the sky.

After comprehensive renovation and restoration work was carried out in the middle of the 1990s and again in 2007/2008, cultural events, alongside a few religious celebrations, now take place in the unfinished church, from theatre performances and open-air concerts to the traditional Mallorquin dance events in summer. Then the large lawn is fitted out with chairs and the unfinished church becomes, without further ado, an open-air stage.

Address Plaça de Sant Ignasi, 07550 Son Servera, info at town hall, +34 (0)971 567002 | Getting there From Palma on the Ma-15 to Manacor to Sant Llorenc des Cardassar, then on the Ma-4030 to Son Servera | Hours Always open during the day, usually open in the evening | Tip There is also a gigantic, uncompleted church ruin in Binassalem. It's worth taking a closer look at this unbelievable building that you can't enter, but can view from the outside.

108 The Reservoirs

Cúber and Gorg Blau for Mallorca's drinking water

Up here on the 1,445-metre-high Puig Major, the biggest massif in the Tramuntana mountain range, you will encounter the two large reservoirs Cúber and Gorg Blau. They sit within the landscape as if they had been here for millions of years. But the lakes, the smaller Cúber and two kilometres further down the larger Gorg Blau, were created artificially (Mallorca has no natual rivers or lakes). In the 1970s, after decades of planning, the appropriate valleys were dammed and flooded, to supply the city of Palma with drinking water. The metropolis, as well as other regions of Mallorca, has struggled time and again with water shortages in the course of the tourism boom in the summer months.

The picturesque reservoirs are fed by the numerous mountain streams from the Tramuntana mountain range, especially from Puig Major. In addition there is the rainfall in autumn and winter, which can be quite strong, as well as the annual snowmelt. The two lakes are connected with each other. If Gorg Blau contains too much water, it flows off into the Cúber. The clear mountain water gets to Palma via an elaborate system of water pipelines, partially through tunnels. In the summer months, when lots of water is used by tourism and recently especially through the running of numerous golf courses and wellness spas, water levels drop accordingly.

The atmosphere high up by the two reservoirs is a real contrast to the beach and sea vibe. Surrounded by colossal rock formations, small holm oak forests and lush vegetation down to the water, you are enveloped by deep silence. The long-distance trail GR 221 passes by both lakes, and those who wish to leave the car behind and get to the reservoirs under their own steam, can do so. The banks of Cúber can be reached through a small wooden gate, and Gorg Blau can be walked around in one-and-a-half hours, but sturdy shoes are highly recommended.

Address 07315 Son Torrella (Escorca) | Getting there You reach the reservoirs on the Ma-10 from Sóller via Fornalutx to Son Torella or from Pollença via Lluc | Tip The fixed-wall snow houses for the collection and storage of snow and the production of ice on the Ses Voltes d'en Galileu path from Cúber to Lluc monastery in the Tramuntana range are a real attraction. The Cases de Neu were abandoned with the introduction of electric freezing plants (ruins of snow houses on the long-distance trail GR 221). For hikers: nowadays there are a few dozen 'Refugios', cheap serviced and self-catering huts in the Tramuntana mountain range.

109_ The Catalina Tiles

Commemoration of a saint

You encounter Catalina Tomàs in Valldemossa at every turn. She is omnipresent and the patron saint of the city, although no one can say exactly how she actually operated. Some say she had visions, and was visited by devils and angels. For others she was ecstatically religious, but she is also believed to have performed numerous miracles. She constructed an altar in front of the gates of the town, at which she prayed relentlessly. She was definitely an engaging character and led a life in deep piety, word of which quickly spread.

Catalina Tomàs was born in 1531 as the daughter of a farmer at Carrer Rectoria 5. The small house was converted into a walk-in chapel, which is usually open. The way there leads through the wonderfully laid out and beautifully planted alleyways of the lower village. At just 21 years old, Catalina Tomàs joined the Augustine convent of Santa Maria Magdalena in Palma, where she lived until her death in 1574. Her body lies in state in a glass coffin in the Santa Maria Magdalena church there.

Revered beyond her death by the Mallorquins, and beatified in 1792 by Pope Pius VI, she was canonised in 1930 by Pope Pius XI. Today, she is the only Catholic saint on Mallorca and greatly revered. In honour of their 'La Beata', as she is called in Valldemossa and on the island, the Carro Triomfal, a large procession, during which a six-year-old girl represents Saint Catalina, is held every 28 July.

If you look carefully, you'll see that all through the village there are colourful tiles on the houses, which tell episodes from Catalina Tomàs' life, her mysterious appearances and the popular legends about her. Her memorial stands in front of the Gothic parish church Sant Bartomeu of Valldemossa, and the certificate of her beatification is kept inside.

She is immortalised in a picture high above the altar in the church of the former Carthusian monastery.

Address Carrer Rectoria 5, 07170 Valldemossa | Getting there From Palma on the Ma-1110 | Hours The chapel is always open during the day. | Tip In the Centro Cultural Costa Nord (Avinguda Palma 6), initiated by the actor Michael Douglas, homage is paid to the Austrian Archduke Ludwig Salvator and his boat *Nixe*.

SANTA CATALINA THOMAS PREGAU PER NOSALTRES

110__Chopin's Piano
The true instrument of the brilliant composer

Somehow, when entering the former Carthusian monastery in Valldemossa, visitors sense that it can get really damp, cold and uncomfortable here in winter. This must have been toxic for the lung diseased Frédéric Chopin. And to add insult to injury, the composer didn't even have his own piano to start with – customs had impounded it on its way from Paris. As composing was what kept him alive, he first had to put his masterpieces on paper with an out of tune instrument borrowed from an island neighbour. And when the 26-year-old Chopin strolled through the village with his partner, French author George Sand who was almost 10 years his senior, and her two children, people treated them distantly and with suspicion. The artist couple stayed here for less than two months. At first they were reconciled by the beauty of the landscape and the curative climate, but abandoned ship after six weeks of what seemed to them like the unending winter of 1838/39. He composed his '*Raindrop' Prelude* here, she wrote her bestseller *A Winter in Mallorca* about their short stay. But for what had been to this point a rather sleepy Valldemossa, the uninvited guests became a stroke of luck. The former monastic cells 2 and 4, in which the romantic couple lived and worked, became an attraction after their departure, and the piano left behind by the brilliant composer became a magnet for the public.

But which piano was his? For decades legions of visitors and Chopin lovers paid homage to the wrong instrument. The rooms of the charterhouse, privatised in the course of secularisation in 1835, actually belonged to different families, who converted them into guest accommodation. These were rented by artists who still own them today. It wasn't until 2011 that it was decided by law that the piano from the 'Pleyel' company now exhibited is the instrument on which Chopin composed his immortal music.

Address Sa Cartoixa, Plaça de la Cartoixa 11, 07170 Valldemossa, +34 (0)971 612106 | Getting there From Palma on the Ma-1110 | Hours Summer: Mon–Sat 9.30am–6.30pm, Sun 10am–1pm; winter: Mon–Sat 10am–4.30pm; in summer there are concerts several times a day between 10.30am and 6pm | Tip The charterhouse also contains the old monastery pharmacy, which was still open to villagers until 1913, a treasured library and the 15th-century printing press, and are all highly recommended, as well as a visit to the monastery church and the associated museum.

111__ The Rotonda

Roundabout art is evermore eye-catching

Art on roundabouts is very much in. This is no different on Mallorca. In fact, here it is all the more impressive, as there is barely a single *rotonda* left on the island that hasn't been furnished with some kind of original design. The roundabout is actually a successful way to exhibit art permanently and visibly to everyone and to consume it, so to speak, in passing. There are abstract pieces, realistic things, scenes from everyday life, intricate and bombastic works. And if there's a particular installation you like especially, why not just do a couple of rounds, before turning off onto your planned route?

The creators of most of these works of art cannot be identified, since there is no information on what is behind the individual installations on the roundabouts themselves. It would of course be hard to read such information while driving anyway, not to say somewhat dangerous! It would therefore be all the more interesting if there was a list of the *rotondas*, as many of these works of art are much more than just decoration for the untouched middle of a roundabout.

On the Ma-15 from Palma to Manacor there's a roundabout that is particularly eye catching: at Vilafranca de Bonany on the junctions to Petra and Felanitx. Out of the blue, over-sized people milled from steel, men and women alike, moving with raised hands positioned as if to dance ballet, with two faces, partially painted, juxtaposed in different postures and yet harmonically corresponding. *Ball de Cultures* is the name of this captivating installation from 2005 by the artist Miguel Sarasate, born in Saragossa in 1952, and living and working in Artà since 1970. And there is more art in public space by him. The sculptor created a six-metre-tall sculpture group called *Guards of Canyamel* on the road Ma-4042 from Artá to Canyamel for example, just before the Torre de Canyamel.

Address Ma-15 Rotonda Petra / Felanitx, 07250 Vilafranca de Bonany | Getting there
On the Ma-15 between Vilafranca de Bonany and Manacor | Tip You can visit the artist's
studio by appointment (Miguel Sarasate, Carrer / Son de Son Servera 63, 07570 Artà,
+34 (0)689 298112).

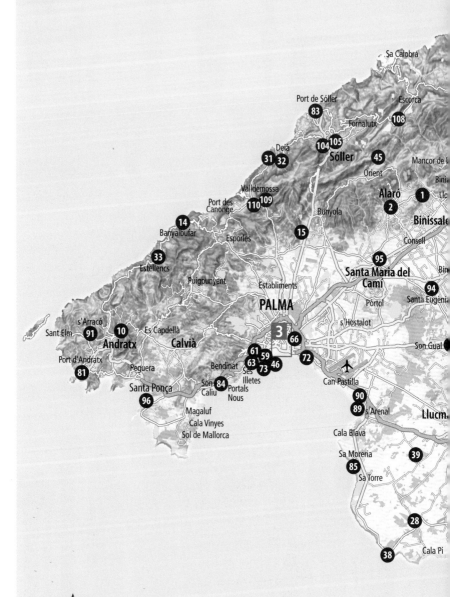

1

Sa Calobra

Port de Sóller
83

Escorca
108

Fornalutx

Deià
31 **32**

104 **105**
Sóller

45

Mancor de l

Orient

Bini

Valldemossa

110 **109**

Alaró
2

1

Llc

Binissale

Port des
Canonge

Bunyola

Consell

14

Banyalbufar

Esporles

15

Santa Maria del
Camí
95

Bin

33

Estellencs

Puigpunyent

Establiments

94

Santa Eugènia

PALMA

Pòrtol

s'Hostalot

Son Gual

s'Arracó

91

Sant Elm

10

Andratx

Es Capdellà

Calvià

3 **66**

72

Port d'Andratx

81

Peguera

Bendinat

61
63 **59**
73 **46**

Son
Caliu

84

Ses
Illetes
Portals
Nous

Can Pastilla

Santa Ponça

96

Magaluf
Cala Vinyes
Sol de Mallorca

90
89 s'Arenal

Llucm

Cala Blava

Sa Moreria

85

Sa Torre

39

28

38 Cala Pi

N

0   4 km

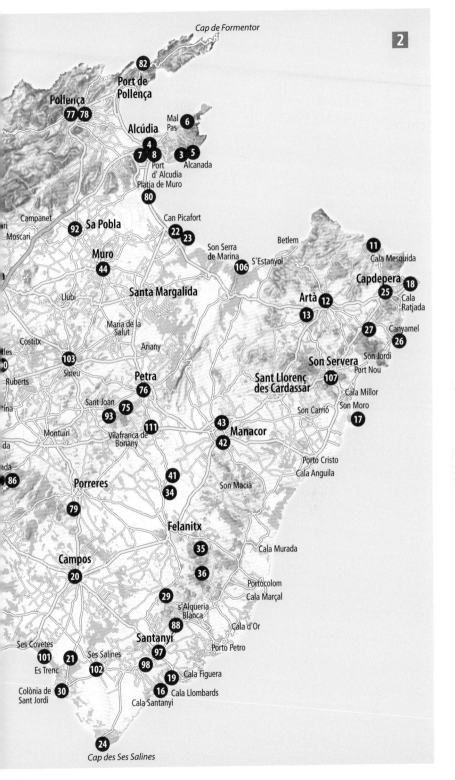

Rüdiger Liedtke
111 Places in Munich
That You Shouldn't Miss
ISBN 978-3-9545-1222-5

Kay Walter, Rüdiger Liedtke
111 Places in Brussels
That You Shouldn't Miss
ISBN 978-3-7408-0259-2

Laszlo Trankovits,
Rüdiger Liedtke
111 Places in Cape Town
That You Must Not Miss
ISBN 978-3-95451-610-0

Laszlo Trankovits
111 Places in Jerusalem
That You Shouldn't Miss
ISBN 978-3-7408-0320-9

Andrea Livnat,
Angelika Baumgartner
111 Places in Tel Aviv
That You Shouldn't Miss
ISBN 978-3-7408-0263-9

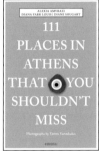

Alexia Amvrazi,
Diana Farr Louis, Diane Shugart,
Yannis Varouhakis
111 Places in Athens
That You Shouldn't Miss
ISBN 978-3-7408-0377-3

Rolando Suárez
111 Places in Gran Canaria
That You Shouldn't Miss
ISBN 978-3-7408-0604-0

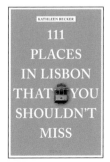

Kathleen Becker
111 Places in Lisbon
That You Shouldn't Miss
ISBN 978-3-7408-0383-4

Catrin George Ponciano
111 Places along the Algarve
That You Shouldn't Miss
ISBN 978-3-7408-0381-0

Thomas Fuchs
111 Places in Amsterdam
That You Shouldn't Miss
ISBN 978-3-7408-0023-9

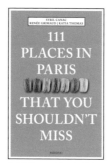

Sybil Canac, Renée Grimaud,
Katia Thomas
111 Places in Paris
That You Shouldn't Miss
ISBN 978-3-7408-0159-5

Irène Lassus-Fuchs,
Julian Spalding
111 Tastes of Paris
That You Shouldn't Miss
ISBN 978-3-7408-0581-4

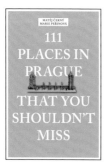

Matěj Černý, Marie Peřinová
111 Places in Prague
That You Shouldn't Miss
ISBN 978-3-7408-0144-1

Jan Gralle, Vibe Skytte,
Kurt Rodahl Hoppe
111 Places in Copenhagen
That You Shouldn't Miss
ISBN 978-3-7408-0580-7

Kai Oidtmann
111 Places in Iceland
That You Shouldn't Miss
ISBN 978-3-7408-0030-7

John Sykes, Birgit Weber
111 Places in London
That You Shouldn't Miss
ISBN 978-3-95451-346-8

Nicola Perry, Daniel Reiter
33 Walks in London
That You Shouldn't Miss
ISBN 978-3-95451-886-9

Kirstin von Glasow
111 Gardens in London
That You Shouldn't Miss
ISBN 978-3-7408-0143-4

Laura Richards, Jamie Newson
**111 London Pubs and Bars
That You Shouldn't Miss**
ISBN 978-3-7408-0893-8

Emma Rose Barber,
Benedict Flett
**111 Churches in London
That You Shouldn't Miss**
ISBN 978-3-7408-0901-0

Ed Glinert, Marc Zakian
**111 Places in London's East
End That You Shouldn't Miss**
ISBN 978-3-7408-0752-8

Martin Booth, Barbara Evripidou
**111 Places in Bristol
That You Shouldn't Miss**
ISBN 978-3-7408-0898-3

Kim Revill, Alesh Compton
**111 Places in Leeds
That You Shouldn't Miss**
ISBN 978-3-7408-0754-2

Julian Treuherz,
Peter de Figueiredo
**111 Places in Manchester
That You Shouldn't Miss**
ISBN 978-3-7408-0753-5

Julian Treuherz,
Peter de Figueiredo
**111 Places in Liverpool
That You Shouldn't Miss**
ISBN 978-3-95451-769-5

Michael Glover,
Richard Anderson
**111 Places in Sheffield
That You Shouldn't Miss**
ISBN 978-3-7408-0022-2

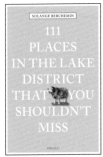

Solange Berchemin
**111 Places in the Lake District
That You Shouldn't Miss**
ISBN 978-3-7408-0378-0

Katherine Bebo, Oliver Smith
111 Places in Poole
That You Shouldn't Miss
ISBN 978-3-7408-0598-2

Alexandra Loske
111 Places in Brighton and
Lewes That You Shouldn't Miss
ISBN 978-3-7408-0255-4

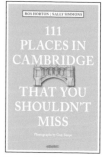

Rosalind Horton,
Sally Simmons, Guy Snape
111 Places in Cambridge
That You Shouldn't Miss
ISBN 978-3-7408-0147-2

Justin Postlethwaite
111 Places in Bath
That You Shouldn't Miss
ISBN 978-3-7408-0146-5

Gillian Tait
111 Places in Edinburgh
That You Shouldn't Miss
ISBN 978-3-95451-883-8

Tom Shields, Gillian Tait
111 Places in Glasgow
That You Shouldn't Miss
ISBN 978-3-7408-0256-1

Gillian Tait
111 Places in Fife
That You Shouldn't Miss
ISBN 978-3-7408-0597-5

Jo-Anne Elikann
111 Places in New York
That You Must Not Miss
ISBN 978-3-95451-052-8

Floriana Petersen, Steve Werne
111 Places in San Francisco
That You Must Not Miss
ISBN 978-3-95451-609-4

Laurel Moglen, Julia Posey,
Lyudmila Zotova
111 Places in Los Angeles
That You Must Not Miss
ISBN 978-3-95451-884-5

Amy Bizzarri, Susie Inverso
111 Places in Chicago
That You Must Not Miss
ISBN 978-3-7408-1030-6

Dave Doroghy, Graeme Menzies
111 Places in Vancouver
That You Must Not Miss
ISBN 978-3-7408-0494-7

Anita Mai Genua,
Clare Davenport,
Elizabeth Lenell Davies
111 Places in Toronto
That You Must Not Miss
ISBN 978-3-7408-0257-8

Benjamin Haas, Leonie Friedrich
111 Places in Buenos Aires
That You Must Not Miss
ISBN 978-3-7408-0260-8

Beate C. Kirchner,
Jorge Vasconcellos
111 Places in Rio de Janeiro
That You Must Not Miss
ISBN 978-3-7408-0262-2

Christoph Hein, Sabine Hein
111 Places in Singapore
That You Shouldn't Miss
ISBN 978-3-7408-0382-7

Christine Izeki, Björn Neumann
111 Places in Tokyo
That You Shouldn't Miss
ISBN 978-3-7408-0024-6

Kathrin Bielfeldt,
Raymond Wong, Jürgen Bürger
111 Places in Hong Kong
That You Shouldn't Miss
ISBN 978-3-95451-936-1

Special thanks to Sofía Dobrzecki and Manfred Marotzke.

Rüdiger Liedtke is the author of the bestseller, *111 Places in Munich That You Shouldn't Miss.* He has known Mallorca for decades. He regularly spends time on the island and is a great fan of the city of Palma. Rüdiger Liedtke lives and works in Cologne, Germany. He has also written '111 Places' guidebooks for Cape Town and Brussels. www.ruediger-liedtke.de